Many thanks to my son Garry, my niece Tracey and my grandson Eddy for their time and effort in helping me put my work together.

British Library Cataloguing In Publication Data

A Record of this Publication is available
from the British Library

ISBN 184685251X
978-1-84685-251-0

Published June 2006 by
Exposure Publishing, an imprint of Diggory Press,
Three Rivers, Minions, Liskeard, Cornwall PL14 5LE
WWW.DIGGORYPRESS.COM

MY FAMILY LINEAGE

Father   -   Alfred, Henry, Bilsby
                       Born: 28th April 1908

Mother   -   Matilda, Anne, Gladys, Irene, Ripley
                       Born: 12th April 1912

Daughter   -   Rebecca Bilsby
                       Born: 29th July 1933

Daughter   -   Mary, Florence, Bilsby
                       Born: 14th November 1934

Son   -   John, Henry, Bilsby
                       Born: 7th March 1936

Son   -   James, William, Bilsby
                       Born: 21st May 1937

Son   -   Robert, Joseph, Bilsby
                       Born: 26th September 1939

Daughter   -   Christine, Anne, Bilsby
                       Born: 15th October 1949

INTRODUCTION

W ho am I? I'm a woman made up of many different things, just like any other woman. But it's the way in which we are put together that makes us individually unique, and therefore each of us; one of a kind.

A Wife; to a good man for twenty-five years – with no regrets.
A Mother; to three sons that I can in all honesty say that I have good and sound reasons to be very proud of.
A Grand Mother; that feels that grandchildren are a gift of love.
A Mother-in-Law; who hopefully knows her place in the order of things.
A Sister; who appreciates greatly the existence of her brothers and sisters, who she can share childhood memories with and know that if we needed each other, not one would turn the other way.
An Aunt and Great Aunt; to numerous nephews and nieces to whom I play my part in passing on our family values.

And last, but not least, because without them I would not exist, I am a daughter of a loving father and Mother.

Who am I?

My name is Rebecca and I was born in 1933. My life begins in humble dwellings in the borough town of St. Leonard's On Sea, East Sussex. I am of true Romany descent and found it impossible to trace back more than a few generations because births and even deaths were very often not registered.

I have three sons, as different as the Sun from the Moon and the Moon from the stars; obviously they will play a major role in my life story. I read somewhere that every single person has at least one good story in them, just waiting to emerge as a book that could be of interest to many people.

The youngest of my sons is Darran. His usual time to visit me is on Sunday afternoon. He was sitting with me while I was talking of some of my past experiences, and he wistfully pleaded with me to put pen to paper; if not for the reading people of this world, would I do it for him? He claimed that when I was gone from this life, he wanted something he could reflect upon, a part of me that could remain with him always. So if I am to humour him, I should probably go as far back in my life as it is possible for me to remember, my long-term memory is as vivid now as if it all only happened yesterday, whereas my short term memory is inclined to be rather hit and miss.

So I shall begin at the tender age of four years old.

CONTENTS

CHAPTER ONE

War Declared

The year is 1937, just two years prior to the outbreak of World War II and I'm just four years old. I can't remember too much of these two years, but just for the record I already had a younger brother and sister. I was very happy at this stage of my life; maybe that's why I don't remember much of these two years. However I do remember one occasion very vividly and the mental scars stayed with me for the whole of my life. Visualise with me if you can, my skipping along happily a few feet in front of my Mother, in a pretty floral dress, my hair black and straight, cut just below the ears and worn with a straight fringe. The big black dog that was always sitting outside of our local pub dashed across the road, ran up my back, and brought me down with a great thud; I can still feel its warm breath on my neck, and the terror that filled me. I can remember my Mother picking me up, making soothing noises, and the feeling I had of being as one with her as she held me close to her body. It's the only thing that stands out in my mind at that stage of my life. I think it was the sheer terror of the experience that imprinted it so strongly on my mind. So other than that, it must have been a very happy time for me. But all that was to drastically change.

I remember the first time (I was then six years old) that I heard the eeriest sound I'd ever heard. It vibrated all around me. It was the warning siren for everyone to take cover; war had come to disrupt my idyllic world. There was panic everywhere; people running in all directions, traffic bumper to bumper, to me seemed to be moving at a snail's pace because there were so many vehicles. You must realise at that time the traffic congestion was nothing like the congestion we get now. I remember my father pushing his way through the traffic to get to me. I had been sent with an older child to collect fish and chips for the family's lunch. I remember him shouting to me, "No!" but I couldn't remember what for until a later date.

Apparently I was dashing back to the shop because I had forgotten my Dad's change.

We had a lovely little whippet dog; she was small and sparky, her name was Trixie. She was full of character, we all loved her and she was Dad's trusty pal. Trixie always collected Dad's daily paper from the nearby newsagents. In all the confusion she was hit by a car, with the 'daily' still firmly in her mouth. When Dad found her, a neighbour was kneeling down beside her, he said to my father: "She won't let the paper go Alf." Dad stroked her head and said: "Okay old girl," and Trixie let it go. I never saw her again after that. I never had to be told anything was wrong. Dad's face and the tears streaming down it, said it all. During my lifetime, the only time I saw my Dad cry was when he lost a dog. My Dad was what you would call a man's man, you know, 'men don't cry brigade'. He was tough, but he grieved for his dogs unashamedly.

I knew something unusual was happening; there was much shouting and confusion. I confess I had no idea what all this meant, but I was to realise very quickly. There was fear imprinted on everyone's face. I heard Dad say to my Mum,

"It's finally happened love, and there's no way we can avoid it now. The time has come to fight; war has been declared".

CHAPTER TWO

The Air Raid Shelter

It was dark, it was damp, there were candles; though only two, because it was too risky to allow any light to escape the enclosure. It was a small dugout as it was referred to then, because it literally had been dug out with the help of pick and spade. It must have taken some time. Its location was in the scrap metal yard, just around the corner from where we lived. Uncle Alf and Auntie Becky (she was my Mum's sister), they owned a scrap metal business. They had a young growing family of their own. So we were packed in this dugout quite tightly. On this occasion I didn't know what was going on outside, although I remember feeling anxious and curious as only a child can. But because I was with Mum and Dad and packed like a sardine in a can, I felt secure and safe enough. My second experience was not so fortunate.

Dad must have been at work, so Mum was at home alone with us kids. There was hardly any warning this time, and then I heard it. That heavy droning sound, which could only have been made by many aeroplanes loaded with bombs, not forgetting the added noise of the warning siren. Mum grabbed us and pushed us one by one into the cupboard under the stairs. That's when I realised there was another addition to the family, because she was struggling to get a small pram into the cupboard with us, but there was not enough room. Mum grabbed the baby and kicked the pram away and closed the cupboard door. I remember her mumbling quietly, "It's alright my darlings, Mummy's got you safe."

"What's that noise Mum?" I asked.

"Not to worry," she replied, "It's just the pictures falling off the wall and tumbling down the stairs." I remember thinking, that's a lot of noise for just a few pictures falling down.

"Mum, why are you crying?"

"I'm not crying darling."

11

"Yes you are," I said. "Your tear just dropped down onto my knee."

"Hush darling. Just cuddle up close to Mummy, Daddy will be here soon." She must have been terrified. The noise had all stopped but still we sat there. I think now that she was probably waiting for my Dad.

When we eventually emerged, it was to find that our back scullery was no longer there. Pictures indeed had fallen off the walls, everything was in disarray, and a thick layer of dust and bits of rubble strewn everywhere. My Mum, for all her life was known for her continuous dedication to house care: polishing furniture and washing curtains. Lace curtains were washed and hung back up on a weekly basis, so she must have felt quite sick for what had happened to her clean and neat little home. But she also must have felt very fortunate, because the house at the back of our destroyed scullery was flattened to the ground, and the dear old lady who used to pat me on the head and smile at me as she passed, well, she was no more. But much to our neighbour's amazement, her little budgie was still chirping away, and still safely secure in its cage.

Then of course there were the dreaded Doodle Bugs, V-I's; unmanned bombs that were timed to reach over the English Channel, and then drop indiscriminately where they may. You could hear them coming, and you learnt to recognise them by their unique sound.

When they ran out of power, you'd have a few moments silence. You would stand so still, almost as though you were in some kind of time warp, waiting for the explosion you knew was inevitable. Later were to come the V-II's, but by that time, me and my family were on our way to Wales as evacuees, and so escaped that particular horror.

CHAPTER THREE

The Hop Gardens

Dad was waiting for his call up papers, but as yet, there was no sign of them.

"Right!" he said, "I'm taking you lot out of all this; we're going to the Kent Hop Gardens, away from Hastings," my hometown, which is situated right on the south coast.

"What are we to do there Dad?" I asked.

"What we will do my darling is this. We will pick hops for the farmer, who in turn will pay us for the pleasure".

For a while we were safe; or so we thought!

Hop Gardens from the air was thought to look like camouflage, because we were quite often the targets for planes coming back from a raid on London. They obviously decided to drop any ammunition they had left, rather than take it back with them. It was not unusual for me to be grabbed and practically thrown into a ditch of stinging nettles. Fortunately I was lovingly treated with Doc Leaves after the fuss had all died down. Amazingly everyone just dusted themselves down and went straight back to their bins and continued picking hops, almost as if nothing had happened. It seemed as if this was becoming a way of life.

One event stands out in my mind. An actual dogfight was taking place in broad daylight, right over the tops of our heads; machine gun fire as both pilots matched their skills, one against the other. Then came the loud shouts as the Nazi plane was brought down. The English pilot did a sort of victory loop and disappeared out of sight; the rest it seemed was down to us.

The 'Pickers' grabbed anything they could lay their hands on that could serve as some kind of weapon. Farm workers with pitchforks were all running towards the plane that was now lying crippled in the middle of a field. They all stopped short a few yards away, ready for battle and to defend their families, including their many young children. This was just a small plane, and as far as I can recall held only one occupant, that being the pilot. He crawled out of the plane and even managed to stand, with his arms held high in the air. He was very young and obviously very scared. He was disarmed, and then walked back to the farmhouse by the workers, and held prisoner until the authorities came and took him away.

Everyone was very quiet that evening huddled around the small campfire. We were watching Mum cooking a meat pudding and dropping lots of spuds and veggies into a big iron pot.

Out of the quiet came the small voice of a young girl called Joan. Her mum had allowed Mum and Dad to bring her with us.

She was in fact our babysitter when we were back home, and what she said must have brought home to everyone in hearing distance the danger that we were all still trying to come to terms with.

"If I am going to die," she said, "I want to die with my Mum. Please take me home". There were tears in her eyes.

Dad made a special trip back with her, and safely handed her over to her Mother. The trip there and back must have taken him at least three hours. I can only imagine his worry and concern to get back to us as soon as he could.

Soon after, we had to get a doctor out to the huts where we lived and slept during the hop-picking season. Dad had broken out in boils, which were situated under his armpits; there were five in all. Three under one arm and two under the other; and when I say boils, I mean boils; they were very large and the doctor had to lance them there and then. Whilst Dad sat alongside the campfire, he must have been in great pain, and I remember thinking how very brave he was. Mother almost fainted; someone had to push her head down between her knees to bring her round.

We stayed the full six weeks picking. It was decided that it was safer than what was happening back at home.

Within days of us arriving back, arrangements had been going ahead for Mum and us kids to be evacuated to somewhere safe. By this time, Dad's call up papers had arrived; he barely had the time to help Mum prepare for this momentous event.

By this time, there was yet another tiny person added to this loving family. So now there was Dad, Mum, myself, Mary, John, James and Robert Joseph. I'm not sure when it became apparent to me that we had all acquired names from out of the bible. There was so much love in this little family and we were about to be split asunder, when I asked, "When will I see you again Daddy?" His reply was very vague.

"I really don't know my darling, but as soon as it is possible, I will find you all". The poor man at that stage wasn't even sure where we were going. He was told he would be informed. We were not to see him again for six months. He had undergone severe training in that time, and he was given a very short two-day leave before being sent into action; and as he promised, he did find us.

CHAPTER FOUR

Evacuation

There we all were, sitting on the railway platform - my mum and her five children, all wearing nametags and a brown box tied by string hanging around our necks. Mother said it was called a gas mask and may one day prove to save our lives. I'm happy to say the time never came for us to wear it, but I seemed to be lugging this thing around forever. Everyone was issued with Identity Cards.

Mother said the train had been derailed, but we were not told at that stage that it had actually been bombed, plus, that the rails had been damaged and were in need of repairs. We were meant to go somewhere in Somerset, but instead we were put on a train to Wales. There could not have been time to inform Mother of where we were heading.

Enter now Aunt Tilly. She was a single Mum with one child; a boy, and his name was Danny. She refused to be separated from us. Although she was my Dad's sister, she was very close to my Mum. Our time in Wales proved how supportive they were to each other and how very close indeed they were to become.

While we were all nibbling on some sandwiches Mum had made for the journey, Auntie said to Mother, "They're funny looking sheep Tilly. I've been in Somerset often, but I've never seen sheep that looked like these". Well, I best explain that my Mum's name also being Tilly did from time to time cause some confusion for us all, so at some point it was agreed that Mum would be "Tilly" and Auntie would be "Till". So from that time onward, us children were encouraged to call her "Aunt Till".

We had arrived in Wales, and by this time we had learnt why the sheep were different. Mother had said it was because they were "Welsh sheep darlings," and that was to be the only information on

16

the subject of sheep that we were to receive. We found our way to a small town called Ystradgynlias. Apparently the place had seen nothing of the war of the kind we had experienced at home in Hastings.

Here we were to be met by officials who would then secure some form of housing for us. At this point Mother decided to shop for some food as we were now beginning to feel hungry again. She walked into a grocery shop, with us all trailing behind her, and proceeded to converse with the sales person behind the counter. This was great; he could only speak Welsh, and Mother could only speak English. Mother placed upon the counter all the money that she had, and pointed to various items of food. He looked at us all one at a time, and I think it must have been apparent that we were new arrivals; in fact, the evacuees that they had been told to expect. He pushed the money back towards Mother, and she in turn pushed it back towards him, thinking he hadn't understood her request.

"O, Yes!" He'd understood all right. Again pushing the money back towards Mother, he then proceeded to fill the counter with as much shopping as we could carry. I remember Mum was carrying Robert, who was eleven months old in her arms. He must have decided that he had to help a woman with five children to care for. So, with our tummy's full and happy to have found a sympathetic being of such a generous nature, we eventually found our way to the hall, where there seemed to be much confusion.

The officials were desperately trying to organise and arrange us evacuees into some sort of order. Eventually things got under way, and Welsh families were lining up to take the children who had arrived without their parents (their Dads at war, and their Mums working in factories to help the war effort). They were eager to take these children into their homes to ensure their safety for the duration of the war. But being separated from their parents, it could not have been a very happy time for anyone.

Unfortunately, a Mother with five children was a task too much for any family. Someone offered to take Mother and baby, but I think fear must have been more than apparent on my Mother's face; she clung to us all with a strength I sometimes believe I can still feel. Someone who spoke fluent English bent down and whispered in my Mother's ear, "Don't worry, we will find you somewhere where you will be able to keep your family together".

We were placed in an end-terraced house that was in fact, half a house. One up, one down; there was no room for furniture, a large double mattress placed on the floor filled the upstairs compartment completely. Downstairs had a small black range that gave us a small fire, and hobs to put pans on to cook. With only two small chairs, most of us just sat on the floor. It was meant to be temporary accommodation, but we were there for quite some time.

Aunt Till was found a room with a small kitchenette, and she seemed to settle there quite happily. She wasn't more than a five-minute walk from us. It didn't take her long to find a job, and a babysitter. When the babysitter ever let her down, she would call on Mum, so there were times when Mum had six kids to cope with.

Dad's Royal Marine pay came through with flying colours, and it seemed that everyone had come to terms with their lot. The admiration I held for my Mother, I am unable to put into words. She stayed so close to us kids; she managed, even with all that was happening, to instil in us the feeling of security that young children need to grow healthily.

Outside the half house was a very shallow babbling brook, which us older ones would play in. We could walk across it carrying our shoes, and playing within sight of the house in a large green open field.

Then came the day when Mother informed us that we were to be moved. Well, I can tell you that it didn't take us long to pack; we hardly had anything.

I honestly can't be too sure how Mum had felt regarding this cramped style of living, but for myself, I can only state how happy in my play I had always been there.

Aunt Till

The new accommodation came as a really big surprise; it was in fact a scout's hall. What happened to the poor scouts, I never did find out. I felt sure that they managed to find them alternative premises. The powers that be had done us proud; they had put up partitions that only went upwards half way towards the ceiling, which was to serve us as bedrooms. They had installed a black welsh range that housed a fire and an oven so Mum would at last be able to cook properly; as in roasting. Hobs on top of course, and a brick shelf that went all the way around the sides and back of it. Mum would place odd house bricks there to warm all day in the winter, and then wrap them up in pieces of old blanket and place them in our beds. They would serve as hot water bottles and I promise you; they did the job extremely well.

It was furnished with odd bits of furniture but that didn't matter. At last we had a place that resembled a proper home, and we were still altogether.

The Salvation Army was a blessing at these times. Mum received much help in the form of clothing, and until the day she died, she'd tell us never to pass these people by without putting some money into their collection boxes. She could never praise them enough. There was also the Women's Volunteer Service; they were another source of help. It made no difference to children, the fact that they were wearing out their clothes faster than their share of clothing coupons could supply. All that kind of worry fell totally on the shoulders of parents. Women were expected to knit socks, which would be sent to men on the front line of battle. Mum had little time to spare, but she did manage when she was able to get the wool to knit. Unfortunately, her efforts for the war were in vain because when she ever finished a pair; one of us kids was in need. It was probably just as well, because Mum always managed to make a hash of turning the heel, which would enable the sock to fit the foot comfortably. But Mum always did her very best.

I must not fail to mention that this new home of ours was smack bang in the middle of Sir and Lady Gilbertson's Estate with thoroughbred horses, boating lake and trout fishing. Sir Gilbertson would often bring Mum half a dozen trout, when he'd been fishing.

"That will help to fill the little one's tummies up I'm sure," he would say, and it was indeed a great help to Mum because now we had ration books.

Banana was the fruit that we all missed. Mum would send me to the shop to queue when the news went out that the banana boat had got through. I think now how brave these men were. Ships were regularly bombed, and not many got through; some didn't even attempt to try. So I would patiently queue at the local shop only to come back with two bananas.

"Did you tell the shop keeper that there are six of us?"

"Yes," I said. But it didn't matter; that's all I could get.

"Well," Mum said, "a taste is better than none".

She did the weekly shopping in town, and when she returned she would put away the goods, then clear the table and proceed to tip out the bag of toffees. She always brought us toffees; they lasted longer, she would say. We would all stand around the table with our hands clasped behind our backs while she counted them out, one by one, until there was a little pile in front of each of us. "Okay," she'd say "Away you go".

We would grab our share of toffees and find a quiet spot and proceed to consume our feast as slowly as we possible could. I always saved my favourite until last; but doesn't everyone!

Lady Gilbertson would hold garden fetes. It was 1940 - I was seven. All the ladies were wearing long colourful dresses and quite large hats. I'm sorry to say I can't remember what the gentlemen were wearing, but these fetes were held I believe to raise funds for charity. Us kids would climb onto the five bar gate and watch these colourful events in progress. At the end, we would be invited to climb over the gate and have a go at the Lucky Dip.

It was always a cause for concern for Mum being on trust on this wonderful property. Keeping five kids in line must have been a full time job on its own.

The Welsh people were very good to us, although in the very beginning there was quite a lot of resentment felt by some of the people. They especially didn't take too well to London women who proved to be too free spirited for Welsh women and their way of life. Welsh women then, were not allowed in pubs; it just wasn't acceptable. The only time that they went anywhere near a public house was Sunday lunchtime to the back door, carrying a large jug that the publican would fill with Ale for the Sunday lunchtime table. So, it's not too difficult to imagine the disapproval of these ladies, knowing that evacuee women were inside the pub with their men enjoying a good old sing song. Over a period of time, Mum was to earn their respect in many ways, other than not entering into pubs. A turning point was when my brother, John, who was a child himself, threw himself over a Welsh neighbour's two-year-old child to protect her from some Shire horses that had escaped their enclosure, and were galloping across a play area. John received a light gash on the back of his head as one of the Shires attempted to clear him. John was proclaimed a hero and lived on this special attention for some weeks. It seems from that time onward, we were all to enjoy a very good relationship with these people, and who were genuinely sad to see us go when the war came to an end.

Aunt Till even ended up marrying one. He was a very quiet man, but Auntie was very happy and in love.

My education though, was the thing that suffered, and I don't believe I ever quite caught up with it. When I did return to Hastings at the age of twelve, I was well behind my fellow classmates and worked reasonably hard to make up for my lost English lessons.

Now peace again was with us. During my five years in Wales, I only remember seeing my Dad a few times. He said he was lucky to have survived the war; so many of the men he knew had died.

He claimed that whenever volunteers were called for, they refused to take him because he had five children, but never the less he did see action, and did his bit for King and Country. He was always so very proud to be a Royal Marine. In our last two years in Wales, Mum made her one and only visit home to her family. She travelled on her own, which in it's self was a new experience for her. She stayed over night and travelled back the next day.

She actually spent very little time with loved ones in her anxious need to return to us; we had been left with very kind and good neighbours. Mum brought back with her great bars of 'Black Market' chocolate. We never had such a feast as we had that day. She also brought back a radio; it was something that I couldn't even remember seeing or hearing before. It must have taken great effort on her part to travel with such a heavy package. Mum placed it on the sideboard and we all pulled up chairs to be close to this unusual contraption. Unfortunately, the sound knob must have been on full. When she switched the radio on, it was the first time I had ever heard the voice of Winston Churchill, the blast of his booming rhetoric sent me falling off my chair and gave us all the fright of our lives. Once we got ourselves back to normal, this radio was to be a source of entertainment for us all, especially for our Mum. We would hear Vera Lynn with hit songs, such as "There'll be blue birds over the white cliffs of Dover"; she was the force's favourite. There was Gracie Fields singing songs like, "Sally Sally, pride of our alley," and "Wish me luck as you wave me goodbye". She was a real favourite with the factory workers. Other songs that stood out in my mind were "Pack up your troubles in your old kit bag and smile boys, smile," and "Yes, we have no bananas, we have no bananas today". Also, "You are my sunshine, my only sunshine – you make me happy when skies are grey". There was of course many more. Many can be heard on the TV series 'Dad's Army', portraying how the Home Guard played a very important roll on the home front. I've lost count how many repeats of this series have been shown, but they are still enjoyed to this very day by thousands.

Mum always claimed she was just too busy with us five kids to ever feel lonely, but I'm sure she must have missed Dad and worried constantly about his safety, but she never allowed this to come across to any of us.

Although I missed Dad terribly, I have to say that our time in Wales with Mum in this safe haven was again, very happy times.

23

The Welsh authorities offered us Welsh Citizenship because we had been there for five years. Mum thanked them profoundly but claimed it was now time for us to go home. We only had to wait for Dad to be de-mobbed; eventually he arrived. He stayed a few days only, and then left ahead of us to acquire some kind of home for us to live in. So, once again Mum set off on the homeward journey with the five of us in tow, with a promise from Aunt Till that she would follow sometime not in the too distant future. I can state that some months later, along with Danny and her new husband, plus a brand new baby boy named Roy, she did indeed follow. Our time spent in Wales was behind us, and yet another new adventure awaited us in Hastings. We still had ration books, but what did that matter; we felt safe because the war was now over.

Me and My Sister Mary

CHAPTER FIVE

D-Day

The horrors of war Dad would not relate to us children until we were much older.

As a Royal Marine, he spent time on a ship named the HMS Furious. Whilst under attack he was to experience his first real taste of war. But for the most part he was placed at various points on our own shorelines, ready for any invasion that may have been planned for us by our enemies.

When he spoke to me of D-Day, he would get quite choked up with emotion. People, he said, talked about D-Day as if it had been a great success. Dad claimed it had been a shamble. Anything that could have gone wrong, did.

Yes, France was liberated and the war moved on to its final conclusion, and victory was ours. But the price was paid in human lives that day. Thousands died with thousands of casualties. Dad told me, it must never be allowed to be forgotten. I know now he was granted his wish. There has been a great deal written on the subject of World War II.

We must never forget those that gave so much, so that we all could once again enjoy the freedom that is so rightly ours.

CHAPTER SIX

Celebrating Peace

It's 1945 and I'm now twelve years old. All five of us were able to settle in a school, which gave Mum more time to herself, but not much. There was always plenty for her to do: cleaning, cooking, mending our clothes; a very necessary task as we still had clothing coupons. Mum often made trousers for the boys out of our old coats. Nothing was wasted. Dad was given a job in Uncle Alf's scrap yard.

Mum, having seen us safely off to school, took on a job herself, two hours a day, five days a week cleaning and washing up for a small guest house near by. Money was very scarce; there was no such thing as a Social Security Department to help us, only the poor house. But Mum's endeavours paid off because two years later Dad started up a metal scrap yard of his own and things gradually improved.

There were street parties. The first was to celebrate the return of loved ones, and the peace that had so painfully been paid for in the loss of husbands, fathers, sisters, brothers, sons and daughters. Even at my tender age, I was very much aware of how lucky in that department we had been.

A great delight for us was the seaside. I hadn't been near the sea since I was four. We even had the pleasure of toys; denied to us in Wales, simple in design and costing very little. My two favourites; one being the 'hoop and stick', which you set the hoop off rolling and then ran alongside and beat it with a stick to keep it going for as long as you could (a great form of exercise for all). The second was the 'whip and top'. Again, you set the top spinning and with the whip you lashed at it, sending it spinning in leaps and bounds, and ran alongside of it to keep it going – great fun.

My brothers played with marbles, jacks and the ever-faithful football. If and when lucky, a few lead soldiers. To think such simple toys could give us so much pleasure. The expectations of today's young children I sometimes find quite alarming.

Another very evident fact was the missing iron railings and gates that had been torn down and given to factories for the war effort. And, I firmly believe this was all done voluntarily. I can well imagine armoured vehicles, guns, possibly tanks, even ships being built in part by all this melted down iron and metal, which proved how people worked together here at home to help our men and women fighting for peace and victory and an end to a terrible war. The Identity Cards we had once been issued were abolished in 1952.

Over a period of time, the rationing slowly disappeared from our lives. The coupons that stand out in my mind were the sweet coupons. Radio announcements were sent out asking everyone not to panic; there were plenty of sweets now for all. But the public played very little heed to this request, including yours truly.

There were queues that lined up all along the road at every sweet shop in our area. Shops were being replenished on a daily basis and this constant demand continued for some weeks, but eventually people realised that, yes, there was no need to panic and slowly the queues began to diminish. The shopkeepers must have made a small fortune at this exciting time.

Much effort was made to rebuild all the damage done by the bombing. Though money was scarce for most, there was a noticeable lifting of spirits as everyone went about their daily lives. We had paid a terrible price for peace and were learning to live again; putting as much of the stress of the war behind us that we could. Memorials were set up everywhere, so that the sacrifices made by those that had died for us could always be remembered.

My sister Mary and I joined the Girl Guides, and my three brothers joined the Scout Cubs. I now know that this gave Mum and Dad a couple of hours privacy at least once a week, so it will come as no surprise when I tell you Mum was delivered of a little girl named Christine Anne. That was to be our family complete.

Mum said that Dad missed out on all of us five when we were tiny children, so this latest addition was to fill that gap; but Chrissy did much more than that. She was a delight for us all. Never had a child received so much love and attention. A child so indulged should have grown up to be a terrible brat, but the never-ending mystery is that she grew to be the most delightful person one could imagine, and I am happy to say, she still is to this very day.

The worst that kids got up to was the ringing of doorbells and scrumping. I can promise you there was not the vandalism that we have today. Neither was it feared to allow a child to take on a paper round. So Dad was quite willing for me to do a Sunday paper delivery. This would be my first experience of pocket money. Shall I tell you what I spent it on? I bet some of you will have a really good guess. That's right, Sweets! I like to think I shared them with my brothers and sisters, but in all honestly I do not remember. I'm not a selfish person, so I like to think that perhaps I did.

My Sister Christine

CHAPTER SEVEN

Brothers & Sisters

Up until now, I have written very little of my brothers and sisters. To me they were my constant playmates, but they are emerging now as much more. To imagine having been an only child is just unthinkable.

Mary was next in line to me; she is just 16 months younger. She spent the first two years of her life in a hospital with Pleurisy and Pneumonia. Mum was told to expect the worst, but she was not to be daunted. Her visits to the local hospital were on a daily basis. At some point in those two years, a film star whose name as far as I can remember was Evelyn Laye, was introduced to Mary as the hospital's miracle baby. As a result of Mary's long hospitalisation, she was very pale and had large brown eyes; she must have looked very appealing. The star asked whether it was possible to adopt her. The doctor declared "not very likely at all; not with this Mother". On the day Mum was to collect her from hospital, and finally take her home, Mum was told she would have to wait a couple of more days, as Mary for the first time in her young life had stood up in her cot, reached upwards and pulled a vase of flowers tumbling down upon her head. But keeping her with them a little longer was a precautionary decision just to ensure no serious damage had been done.

Whilst I always seemed to be hanging around Dad, Mary was really Mum's girl. When her time came to leave school and follow my footsteps by taking a job, she found this very difficult indeed. She would constantly come over nauseous and after some weeks of this, Mum pleaded with Dad to allow Mary to stay at home with her and help with household chores and with baby Chrissy. Dad had expected us children upon starting work to contribute to the family needs, by handing over a part of our earnings. But eventually he agreed to let Mary stay at home, and be of help to Mother.

A Countrywide craze had come, in the way of Bingo! With Mary to baby-sit, Mum trotted off with a neighbour to try her luck. This developed into a once a week trip, which continued until we were very much grown up, at which time Mum started going twice a week. Dad at first had alarm bells going off in his head; was Mum going to turn into a habitual gambler? This of course did not happen; she only found great delight in this new pastime.

As Dad's business grew, he himself started to have a little flutter, as he would call it, on the Gee Gee's. He would read up their form by studying the daily papers.

So, Mary continued at home sharing the bringing up of baby Chrissy. But when Chrissy was about five years old and started school, Mum and Dad tried persuading Mary to take a job. This she did with great effort on her part, and she finally made it.

The catering trade had seemed an uncomplicated choice of work for her, and as time went on she worked her way up to become manageress of the local tea rooms, that were then called 'The Sun Lounge'; its now known as 'The Marina'.

Around about this time, Mum was going through 'the change of life'; her hormones were all over the place. There was little help in those days for women going through this unpleasant ordeal. It was a disturbing time for us all. After all we had gone through together, it seemed that Mum was finally going to be falling apart before our very eyes, but in time it passed. It seems that Mum having Chrissy so late in her life at thirty nine, had played a considerable part in helping her through this most unpleasant time.

At the age of twenty, Mary it seemed was going to get married to a young soldier named Eric. We were all pleased for her; he was indeed a very pleasant and polite young man and we all grew, over the passage of time, to become very fond of him. Before this, however, I was somewhat concerned because I was responsible for the joy of Mary's first experience of love being taken away from her:

a certain very good looking young man who suffered quite severely with consumption, often coughed up blood and who in fact was extremely ill, caught Mary's eye; and she was lost. She was somewhat younger than him, and would seek out his company whenever she could. I threatened to tell Dad if she didn't stay away from him, and though Dad was very loving, he was also a great disciplinarian and ruled the household with a firm hand. So Mary reluctantly paid heed to my firm bidding, and stopped seeing him, and as far as I can tell, I was forgiven for this timely interference in my younger sister's life.

Eric and Mary on their Wedding Day

I now know that Mary's strong affection for her new husband did indeed at some point in time turn into love. Eventually, they were to bring into the world two children; the first, a boy they named Ian, and not long following came Hilary, a beautiful baby girl.

Mary had always been a strong swimmer, and decided she would study at home to fulfil her wish of becoming a Swimming Instructor. This she did achieve and passed the required exams with flying colours. She was responsible for many achievements by her pupils who won Gold, Silver and Bronze medals as a result of Mary's constant efforts to exact as much as possible from her young and faithful charges. Sadly at the age of sixty, she underwent a severe operation with as many as seventy-six stitches, which resulted in bringing her career as a teacher to an end. She has at this moment in time, four grandchildren: two boys by Ian and his wife Teresa, and a boy and girl by Hilary and her husband Steve. Mary is at this very moment of writing my story, flying over to Portugal to spend a week with her son and family, so I will leave her to this special joy and I look forward to her safe return.

Next in line is brother John. All his life it seems he has had this broad grin that would spread across his face and delight all that knew him. He is a somewhat quiet man, very strong in character and very family orientated. He is also now married to a pretty dark haired girl from Tenterden who John had met while on one of the trips to the Kent Hop Gardens. Their courtship was considered to be somewhat unstable; maybe the distance between them proved to cause a bit of strain.

I remember John phoning and sadly informing me that it was all off again. I had already bought, as a likely wedding present, a set of saucepans with lovely bright red lids. So, having been told that this happy event was not to take place, I decided to cook a tasty stew in the largest of these pans. It was simmering merrily along, but then came dashing in my brother John.

"It's on," he proclaimed. "The wedding is next Saturday. Sorry my love," he said "I must dash"; he obviously had a lot to do. I quickly emptied the stew into my old saucepan and spent a good ten minutes cleaning this pan with the lovely red lid, in an effort to bring it back to its original gleaming glory. I always seemed to be buying saucepans as wedding gifts. I think it was linked to the fact I was badly in need of saucepans myself, but there was always something more important to spend my money on.

I remember the mad dash to get to the wedding on time. We were in Dad's car, which was an ageing Humber, but it was kept in pretty good condition. I remember the leather seating and the wooden dash panels. Dad called it 'The old lady'. He would always polish it until it gleamed. On the journey there, (Dad was driving very safely – he was in fact a brilliant driver), he drove the Humber over a humpback bridge just a little too fast which resulted in us all bouncing quite high off our seats. Poor Mum's lovely new hat got flattened by the roof of the car. Mum was somewhat put out by the fact that Dad's concern seemed to be all for the car, rather than her new hat. By the time we arrived (on time I might add), we were all smiling and eager to make this day special for our John, and his lovely bride, Jackie. They have since blessed us with four children; two boys and two girls; Sharon, Mark, Louise and Jason.

As time went by, John took a great interest in cars, especially the vintage variety, and working with Dad in the scrap yard dismantling old and crashed vehicles. He learnt a lot about engines and eventually ended up with his own business repairing cars. He also enjoyed drawing and painting, and painted many good pictures, which he still has in his home to this very day. He suffers quite badly now with Rheumatism in his knees. But whenever I pop in to his place of work, he still has that same old grin that spreads across his face and always stops whatever he's doing to spend a little time with me chatting.

James, now what can I tell you about him? He has always been extremely strong, again a quiet man, but there has always been that air of utter innocence about him. He was always very trusting, but I think some of his life experiences have made him somewhat wiser but thankfully not bitter.

My brother John [left] pictured with a buddy from the Army

His marriage to Hazel has lasted the test of time, and as they only had one child named Derek, their lives together ran reasonably smoothly.

As a child Jimmy had to wear leg irons, which was the way the medical profession would treat limbs that needed straightening. As cumbersome as they must have been for him, the treatment proved successful.

As Derek, his son, grew into a young man, he fell into the wrong company and unfortunately became involved with drugs. This caused much distress and pain for many years. So unfair it seemed, as he was their only child. But they were blessed with a beautiful granddaughter, and she plays a permanent part in their lives, and is the source of much love.

Jim had a small truck and was able to earn a liveable wage doing all kinds of work. He never seemed to mind turning his hand to almost anything, so long as he could earn an honest bob.

Jim and Hazel were able to buy a small house, and it's now completely paid for. They now lead a modest lifestyle and they seem to be able to deal with their problems with a quiet strength and acceptance. Unfortunately, after much trial and effort, the situation regarding their son is still unresolved. But we all live in hope that Derek will come through.

Robert, my youngest brother was considered by Mum and Dad to be a bit of a scallywag - a term used to express a child with a tiny wee devil in him, but this wee devil was completely harmless. I would say myself that he was inclined to be rather boisterous and mischievous, not as quiet as his two brothers. Maybe he felt the need to attract a little attention from us all. He was just nine years old when Chrissy was born and possibly felt his nose put out of joint. If this was the case, it didn't last long because he was just as smitten with this new arrival as the rest of us.

My brother James

When he was about eleven or possibly twelve years old, a farmer from a nearby small holding took Robert to confront Dad complaining he had been caught scrumping his gooseberries. The farmer didn't so much mind him having a good feed, but was angry because of the unripe fruit that had been thrown down into the furrows and wasted. As the farmer had approached Dad with a civil attitude, Dad was more than ready to set matters to rights. Dad made Robert pick up the discarded gooseberries, sat him down on the ground and insisted he ate them. The farmer took pity on him when Robert reached a point of hugging his stomach. Father offered the farmer compensation. With the matter settled, Dad took Robert home with a flea in his ear. Needless to say Robert never went there again. Dad's treatment could sometimes be harsh, but he was always fair.

Robert had an unsuccessful marriage, but eventually met and married Lyn. They had two boys: Matt and Lee. All my three brothers worked with Dad in the scrap yard, but like his brothers, Robert eventually set up business on his own. Prior to that, along with his brother John, he was called to serve his two years conscript in the forces. Jim was not to share this compulsory conscription because of his flat feet and the fact that his lungs were scarred by the Pneumonia he had suffered as a very young man, so he was very disappointed. I think he felt this to be a slight on his manhood. So I would like to state here and now that Jim has grown into a man that we have always been very proud of. There are people who say that conscript would sort out some of our unruly youngsters who indulge in so much crime within our society today.

Robert and his family live in a very nice house some way out of town, and I often travel with Chrissy to visit and enjoy a meal and a chat, catching up with present issues, but also often reflecting on times long gone by. So, I now leave Robert, pouring all his energies as ever into securing the future of his two sons and I have no doubt in my mind that he will succeed.

My Brother Robert

Now Christine-Anne. Having already introduced you to this final addition to the family, it just leaves me with the task of trying to put into words how this little bundle of joy proceeded to wind us all around her little finger.

Whilst we were all considered to be quite an attractive family, Chrissy as a young child, with her pert mouth, large eyes and tight curly light brown hair proved to be irresistible to all. It was a case of "Shirley Temple" move over.

With all the work Mum had to do to keep this little family well fed and clean, and myself in work, Mary had charge of Chrissy a great deal, and one time Chrissy had called her Mum. Mary to this day still seems to treat Chrissy as her daughter, rather than a sister, where as my relationship with her has always been a sister and my love for her has grown stronger with each passing year. She was the apple of Dad's eye and could often be found trailing behind him whilst he went about his daily chores. Sometimes, on a Sunday lunchtime, he would even take her to his little local pub, whilst he chatted and downed a couple of pints of Brown Ale, prior to the family Sunday lunch. This was a meal that everyone was expected to be present for, come what may. I am convinced that this habit played an important part in keeping the family bond, which is still with us all today. Mother also laid the table for a special Sunday tea and the rules were the same, unlike today's habit of grabbing a sandwich and plonking yourself down in front of the telly.

Come then the arrival of television, with its then only one channel, that being of course the BBC. Mum and Dad were some of the first to purchase one. Chrissy would invite all the kids in our immediate area to watch children's hour with her. Mum would look pleadingly at Dad when he came back from the yard to wash and have tea, and would quietly whisper over the children's heads, "It's only for one hour Alf, and then I'll send them all packing". Dad's tolerance continued for some months until slowly the numbers diminished as the neighbours, one by one, became the proud owners of a telly of their own.

There were of course the cinemas, but back then they were called Picture Houses, or "flicks" for short, and the Saturday morning matinee for children, which was a treat awarded to us if we had been well behaved. It would consist of various cartoons, a short film and the eagerly awaited continuation of a weekly serial. The Lone Ranger for example, and his trusty Indian pal Tonto, and his beautiful prancing horse, Silver, that would rear its front legs at the opening of each showing. There was Laurel and Hardy, Charlie Chaplin and many others. Not forgetting the unforgettable 'Keystone Cops'. There was George Formby with his cheeky chappy grin, who would sing cheeky songs such as "You should see the sights I see when I'm cleaning windows," accompanied by the strumming on his Ukulele. I mustn't leave out Old Mother Riley and her daughter Kitty, who were in fact a husband and wife act, and would get themselves into the most alarming, yet very innocent situations.

Mary and I, with Chrissy in the middle holding each of our hands, with a firm promise to Mother to take great care of her, would on a Saturday morning partake of this weekly awaited for pleasure. My brothers would at this stage prefer to go their own way. As we had a choice of two Picture Houses, I really don't remember us ever going altogether. Boys being boys, in answer to a dare, John put Robert (his youngest brother) on his shoulders and wearing Dad's coat and trilby hat proceeded to try and get into the pictures as an adult person. Of course, with all the wobbling about, they were soon discovered and with much laughter on their part were sent off with a flea in their ear.

The smaller of the two Picture Houses was situated in Norman Road, St Leonard's, and was called the Kinima. It had a front main entrance and a rear exit, and I know for a fact that my brothers would sometimes slip into this exit when the performance was over and people were leaving. Once they were inside they could easily slip into the front row seats and see the next showing for nothing. I'm quite sure Mum and Dad never knew of these capers.

The larger of these two Picture Houses was in the main London Road, and it was called 'The Regal'. It was quite posh in comparison with the Kinima, and a very large organ would rise up from the pit in front of the screen, and would entertain us with music popular at that time, prior to the beginning of the performance. There would be two films, along with Path news, and that would be our evening's entertainment. The small film would be the 'B' film, then Path News, along with the crowing cock, followed by the 'A' film, which of course was to be the main feature. If you were lucky, a cartoon would be thrown in for good measure. During the interval, two young females would walk down the aisles carrying a tray with a halter strap around their necks selling ice cream and drinks. At some point in time, the 'Kinima' Picture House was to disappear altogether, but 'The Regal' was transformed into the 'Regal Theatre' and many great artists of the time would appear there. It has since been pulled down, and the building that is there now, 'Ocean House', is used in the main for keeping fit, containing a gym, 'Ocean Fitness'.

As Chrissy grew older, she was to be the only one of us ever to be allowed a two-wheeled bike, but she could only ride it around the yard. Dad was dead against bikes; death traps he called them. Shouldn't be allowed on the road, he'd say. Brother Jim was to be the only one to break ranks; at the age of twenty-five he informed Dad he was buying a motorbike.

Chrissy managed to acquire an uninterrupted education, but she was always adamant about becoming a qualified Hairdresser. She is now a very good one, I might say, since this she stuck with all her working life. In her early teens she fell hook, line and sinker for 'The King' Elvis Presley, and she remains loyal to him this very day, and has a complete collection of his music. The second love of her life came at the tender age of fifteen; his name was Christopher. Much to Dad's surprise the courtship was still thriving when Chrissy was sixteen and a half. I received a phone call from her with a request for me to meet her on a very important matter. We arranged to meet at a certain place on the Hastings seafront; she was already sitting on a bench waiting for me. I had no idea what her problem could be, until I saw her face. This was my baby sister, and she was going to tell me that she was pregnant. My heart went out to her. Chrissy denied any suggestion that she was afraid to go to Dad, only that she knew how much this news would hurt and disappoint him.

Christopher was three years older than Chrissy, but still only nineteen years old. I must give him credit; he had wanted to go to Dad with her, but Chrissy pleaded with him to allow her, along with me to approach Dad first. Well, strike while the iron's hot, so that very evening we waited until Dad had washed and eaten, and stood close together with our arms around each other in front of him, making sure to leave about 4 or 5 feet between him and us. Not because we were afraid, but more to avoid the full blast of his expected anger.

I proceeded to inform him to expect some news that he was not going to be very happy about. He waited, "Well, come on out with it," he said.

"Dad, our Chrissy is pregnant."

Well, the expected blast of anger did not come, instead in a very quiet voice he asked,

"Does your Mother know? If she doesn't, you best tell her." The second question: "Where's Christopher?"

Chrissy in an equally quiet voice answered, "He's coming to see you Dad, tonight after work". And that is what he did, proclaiming his love for Chrissy, and proceeded to ask Dad for her hand in marriage.

Dad tried very hard not to show how hurt and disappointed he was, but Chrissy had indeed been correct in her assumptions regarding her news. So it followed, at seventeen she became a married woman with her son Joseph well and truly on the way. To be followed 13 months later by her daughter Tracey. Too soon after Tracey, she became pregnant again, but because of ill health and with her doctor's approval, the pregnancy was terminated. Some two years later, Chrissy was happy to find herself pregnant with her third child, but it was not to be so; she miscarried. Chrissy was obviously dreadfully upset, and claimed that perhaps God was paying her back for her previous termination.

It was decided by Chrissy, along with her husband to call it a day regarding any additions to their family. I think they made the right decision, as Chrissy never seemed to be overly tough at this time in her life. At one stage, while Chrissy was spending a short term in hospital, Mary approached me with the idea of doing some decorating and spring-cleaning as a surprise for Chrissy when she came back home. I was delighted to be part of anything that would raise Chrissy's spirits up to the bright and happy being she had always been before the termination and miscarriage, which had drained her health and spirit. With Christopher's permission, and I might add, his help re-decorating, the three of us set about starting a transformation which had to be completed in five days. Mary and I bought a new cleaner between us; a strange present you might think, but we knew it would be what she would want. We sat patiently on the sofa and waited. Christopher had left to collect her from hospital; we were so very tired, but no way were we going home until we had seen Chrissy's face when she saw what we had done for her. I certainly feel our efforts played a part in her quick recovery, and she went from strength to strength. I was never to forget the joy she displayed on her arrival home.

With the children now at school, she wanted to get back to work. Eventually she was able to rent a premises already set up as a hairdressers shop. With her natural ability and talent, she built the business up, which helped to raise their family's financial status. At some point in time, she sold, and together they ploughed their resources into purchasing their council home.

Their children were growing up fast, and this little family was very happy with their lot. Chris and Chrissy were now able to enjoy a very happy and lively weekend social life, along of course with the usual upsets and tribulations endured by most. But, sadly this was not to last.

Christopher developed very unpleasant and worrying symptoms, and after a visit to their doctor, they were informed that he did indeed have a heart condition, and he was to lose some weight and undergo surgery in London. This came as a terrible shock to this still young and happy family. The day before the operation, Christopher was to ask what were his chances, and he was told he had a fifty-fifty chance. So Chrissy and their two children; by this time were in their very early twenties, made the journey to London to visit him. They all sat around his bed pouring out their love and encouragement with hugs and kisses. They left for home and waited for the good news. Unfortunately, the following day they were to be told that Christopher had died on the operating table from a massive heart attack. He was only forty-two years old. Their grief was unbearable to watch, but as in all forms of grief you can only 'just be there'.

It will take its course in the measure of time, hence the old saying: 'time heals'. But it proves to be very frustrating for the loved ones who just hover and wait.

Chrissy was never to reach her bed of a night for some time. She would be found in the morning in the sitting room, sitting on the carpet with her head lying on her arms that were spread across the settee, and an empty wine bottle on the floor beside her. With much concern by everyone, this period did pass and it is my belief that the love she shared with her children was the saving grace that brought her out of this stage of her mourning. Chris, Chrissy and the children had always shared a great sense of humour. So, when Chris was buried with his tombstone at his feet, instead of at his head, it brought a smile rather than anger. They were convinced that Chris would definitely have appreciated the deliberate mistake. Apparently the bearers could not manoeuvre the coffin easily, due to the position of the burial plot and the fact that Chris had been a very heavy man.

With a few stumbling blocks this little trio was to survive their grief and become closer than ever. At this moment in time, Chrissy with her children grown up and finding herself in this three-bedroom house, decided to swap for a very nice two-bedroom house. She is still working as a hairdresser, and at the age now of fifty-five, having no inclination for the last fourteen years to enter into any kind of emotional relationship, finds herself completely lost to the charms of Terry. I have only as yet met him a couple of times, and I liked what I saw. They both claim they never saw it coming, and both of them seem to be brimming with a sparkle that can be found with couple's in love.

So, I leave Chrissy with my sincere wishes for her future and a profound hope that along with Terry she will find the happiness that she so richly deserves.

. Christopher and Christine on their Wedding Day

CHAPTER EIGHT

Hop Gardens Revisited

From the age of twelve to sixteen years, Dad continued to take me and the family hop picking in Kent. With six children, holidays were definitely out. The hop-picking period generally lasted six weeks and very successfully served as a holiday, and led to brand new clothes for us to wear on our return to school in the new term. These were very happy and memorable times.

Mum would leave the field an hour before the rest of us to light the fire that Dad had set up earlier that morning, and to prepare the main meal. A big iron pot, oval in shape, would be hung over the fire by a large hook attached to a long pole with side supports. Mum would half fill the pot with water, and while waiting for it to boil, would prepare various root vegetables, including potatoes, then cover them with a large damp tea towel while she popped lean neck of mutton or lamb into the boiling water, along with several onions. She allowed it to simmer for an hour before adding the rest of the ingredients, and then thicken with soup squares and Bisto to produce a very tasty gravy. When you've been out in the field from six in the morning until five in the evening, even though Mum had packed sandwiches and drinks for our lunch, you came back to the huts absolutely starving; and boy did we always enjoy these meals cooked over the open fire. I don't know why, but these meals tasted so different from the ones at home.

After clearing up, we would sit around the fire trying to confirm who had picked the most hops, but mostly we would end up having a singsong and Dad often would play his mouth organ with great gusto. As dusk would start to close in, we would in turn be sent to a hut with a bowl of warm water to wash and prepare ourselves for bed. There were never any arguments, as we were all so very tired. Beds were made of bales of hay provided by the farmer; everyone slept well. I don't know if this was because the beds were extremely comfortable of if we were all just plain exhausted.

Five fifty sharp the next morning, Dad would bang on all the hut doors shouting for us to get up, then proceed to line us up at the cold water tap to wash our face and hands, whilst Mum would be preparing breakfast for us all. By this time, she would have already made sandwiches or rolls for midday lunch. We all had to carry something; there was even a kettle. I don't think my Mum could have coped without her cup of tea.

Mid morning, a local trader would arrive at the gardens with his van and an assortment of freshly baked pies. Dad used to say to us kids, if we all picked hard, he would buy each of us a pie. I'm sure we could smell these goodies long before they reached the gardens. One day to our surprise a hearse arrived in the gardens. I thought someone had died! But no, the pie trader jumped out of the driver's seat and proceeded to ring his usual bell. But the pickers were rather reluctant to buy. Dad was the only one in the family that ate a pie and he informed us that the van had broken down and that the hearse was very clean. It didn't help.

My father hop picking

48

My father with his beloved grey hound Susie

This went on for three days. On the fourth day, when the pie man arrived with his usual transport, pies were in great demand. He said to father, "I can't understand it. My sales plummeted when I used the borrowed hearse".

The measurers would arrive from the farm carrying very large wicker baskets, and relieve us of our hops and mark down how many bushels we had picked. Dad also kept a record; this was done twice a day.

The hops stained your hands, and it would take about a week after the season was over to get your hands back to normal. On one occasion whilst sitting around the camp fire, after having filled our hungry tummies with Mum's 'Joey Grey' (a meal that consisted of potatoes, onions and bacon rashers), my great uncle Sid, who had joined us on this occasion, held up two bullets. "Look what I found in the garden today". We were all rather sleepy and responded with little enthusiasm. He suddenly threw them into the now smouldering fire. Dad yelled to us all to jump and we scrambled in all directions, and waited for the bullets to go off, but all we got was a 'pssst' sound, and Uncle Sid, still sitting at the fireside, was grinning his head off. Having been in World War I, he knew the bullets were completely harmless; we all ended up having a good laugh. Dad had actually called him a few explicit words of his vocabulary.

On Saturdays, we would all have a strip wash and put on our best clothes for the weekly shopping trip into Tenterden. This was looked forward to with great enthusiasm. With the shopping done, we would visit the local pub for a well-earned drink for Dad and Mum, and us kids would be left in the children's room with lemonade and crisps. Saturday was the day that Dad would buy fish and chips for our main meal to allow Mum to be free to see to the washing of clothes ready for the Monday. On one of these trips, poor Mum had a very heavy showing, which of course was the beginning of the 'change of life' for her. She dashed to the loo and having purchased some new white vests for the boys at a very good price, had to unfortunately use two of these to help her predicament. I was very alarmed.

Sunday main meal could be either Rabbit or meat pudding cooked in a cloth and simmered for at least two and a half hours to make sure the meat was tender. At home, Mum always made apple pie for Sunday pudding, but of course it was off the menu when we were hop picking. But sometimes if she could talk us kids into going blackberry picking, with the instructions "don't pick the berries close to ground, in case a passing dog has cocked his leg and wee'd on them," she would make a blackberry and apple pudding, again in a cloth, and would cook it in the big pot. This was a dish to make your mouth water while waiting for it to be served up. My Mum was a plain cook, nothing fancy, but she was very good at what her Mum had taught her. I can't ever remember any complaints, not even from Dad.

Towards the end of the hop picking season, during September, the early mornings could be a little chilly. There was to be no chickening out allowed by Dad, but he did light a bit of a fire in a safe area for us kids to occasionally warm our hands.

It was the early morning dew that would settle on the hop binds, making our hands wet and cold, but by eight o'clock the early morning sun would have warmed us up, and with the usual encouragement from Dad to pick and make up the lost time we were still expected to reach the morning target. And, us kids never forgot the promise that Dad made concerning the pie man's visit.

With the hop season now over, we all had to muck in and help with the clearing up of the area. The huts had to be brushed out, all rubbish collected and put into bags, and everything packed and loaded onto Dad's lorry. Dad would also check that everyone had used the loo. The final job was the filling in of the dug out latrine and, thankfully, he carried out this unpleasant job. Being satisfied that everything had been left tidy for the farmer, we would all pile onto the back of the lorry, and Dad would secure the side flaps. Chrissy would ride in the cab with Mum and Dad, and we were on our way home.

On our arrival home, Dad (with the boys to help) would unpack the lorry and, after cups of tea, biscuits and buns all round, we would set about getting the home in order. Dad would take the boys and go and check the yard and the lock ups to make sure everything was OK for business on the coming Monday. Mum, with us girls would unpack, make beds up and sort out all the dirty washing and lay table for dinner. Then Mum would cook something like mashed potatoes, sausages and baked beans. "Just something quick" she'd say.

Saturday evening, and we would all fall into our beds exhausted. Sunday would prove another busy day for Mum getting all the washing done, and the never-ending supply of meals. I still marvel to this day how on earth my Mother coped with this constant drain on her resources. I only know that she loved us with a passion that could not be compared. There was still the shopping of new clothes for us all to be done, and the preparing of us for school.

I never once in my childhood felt I'd missed out on the sort of holidays that my school friends would talk about. Hop picking for my parents was a source of earning money, but for me it was pure joy, plenty of fresh air and a light tan. You wouldn't have found healthier, happier bunch of kids anywhere.

Sadly hop-pickers were to be replaced by machines. If you were to talk to the older generation, I'm certain that you wouldn't find one person who wasn't sad to lose this means of getting into the country away from it all. But time marches on and nothing can stop progress.

My brother Jim

My Mother Matilda

My father [far left] and my brother John [left]. Measurer on the right with his bag man centre, tallying up the morning's pickings.

Left to right, my brother Robert, aunt Anney with daughters Flo and Kathy, brother Jim, brother John, my father and myself.

CHAPTER NINE

Puberty & Purgatory

I'm now sixteen and working in a local grocery store. After only being there a few weeks, the manager set up a challenge for us all to see who could win a grocery prize. We were challenged to push the sale of Tinned Fish (that was very slightly reduced for the purpose). I set my cap at older female customers, and encouraged them to buy this fish as a special treat for their cats. This in fact boosted my overall sales and I did indeed win my prize, which I very proudly presented to my Mum. As the weeks went by, I ended up chatting with one of the more senior assistants, and I asked why they stamped on the wooden flooring when one of the girls was down in the basement making our morning break cup of tea. She informed me it was to warn the tea maker that the manager was on his way down. Apparently he had wondering hands, and she confirmed that was why I hadn't been included in the rota because I was the new girl. In time, wanting to pull my weight, I insisted on taking my turn and promised to listen for the foot tapping on the floorboards. This proved to be quite successful in the main. But, on a day when it was my turn, I failed to hear the warning and was in the process of emptying the teapot into the sink when who should step up behind me, but himself. He placed his arms around me and held my breasts, remarking, "your growing into a big girl". I emptied the teapot over my shoulder, which gave him quite a soaking. I informed him that if he ever touched me again, I would visit his wife in the flat above the store, and tell her what he had done. It only leaves me to tell you that it didn't take long for him to find the excuse to sack me. I didn't tell Dad why because I feared what he would have done to the said manager. So I decided a change of type of work was called for and took a job as a Waitress in a large guesthouse. The owner and manager was a woman, so I couldn't foresee any problems.

Now I had a regular wage packet, I began to use the public private baths. A towel and soap were provided, and you could shout for more hot or cold water if you required it. Up until then it had always been the big tin bath in front of the fire, as we didn't have the pleasure of a bathroom. Mum and Dad must have felt the relief, as one by one we were able to afford the public private baths. I was working my way through puberty and struggling to achieve just a little freedom from Dad's strict regime, but getting nowhere.

My friends were off partying and dancing, but I had to go straight home after finishing work. Dad bought a piece of furniture made by Grundy that held a radio and record player, to keep us in. It also provided cupboard space for Mum to keep her table linen, drinking glasses, her few pieces of good china and the records. It took pride of place in our small sitting-come-dining room. It was Dad's way of making it tolerable to keep us in. He didn't allow me to wear any kind of make up either.

I was beginning to feel deprived and depressed. I decided I would leave home and get myself a job in London; thereby gaining my freedom.

I gave my younger sister a small amount of money I'd borrowed from Dad to give to him, and I also gave her that week's keep for Mum, and I asked her to say I would phone when I got a job. I never told her where I was going. I bought a single train ticket to Victoria Station and felt quite confident in what I was doing and quite convinced I wouldn't have any trouble getting a job and a place to live. But I was to discover I knew nothing, and was in fact very naïve.

After two days of tramping the streets inquiring for work, my money disappearing fast, sleeping in the toilets at Victoria Station, and beginning to feel afraid, dirty and home sick, I slunk into a train destined for home. I didn't have enough money for a ticket, and when the train pulled into Hastings Station, people were showing their tickets as they were leaving. I went in the opposite direction to the toilets and climbed onto the toilet seat. It was very difficult squeezing out of the very tiny window that would get me to the outside of the station, and I landed hands first and sprained my wrist.

I decided Dad was going to be so cross with me, so I couldn't go home. I walked from Hastings Station to Hollington where my Aunt Till lived. I was tired and hungry and she made me something to eat and drink, and then phoned my Dad. When he arrived he looked pale and worn, and that was the first moment that I realized what my actions had caused. I hadn't phoned in the three days that I'd been gone. It must have been a very anxious time for them both. He was so pleased to have me back; he gave me a big hug and made me vow I would never do anything like that again. When we arrived home, Mum was crying and wanted to know why I did such a terrible thing. Dad said to leave it for now and we would talk on the morrow.

The police had been informed of my safe return. They came to the house and gave me a positive lecture on wasting police time. I think I grew up considerably in those three days. Dad eased up on his restrictions a little, and I believe I eased the path for my brothers and sisters coming up behind me. I also believe I was very lucky; all sorts of misfortune could have befallen me in those three days. Now looking back, I'm at a loss to know how I could have done such a thing to my loving parents. Soon life got back to normal and if anything, I became closer to them.

So much for puberty, it was more like going through purgatory.

CHAPTER TEN

Skeletons in the Cupboard

I would sit at Dad's feet while he sang the old songs that his Mum had sung to him, and he would also tell me stories of his younger days and why I should be proud of the fact that I was a Romany Traveller. I always had known, but never paid much heed to the fact. The idea of being a gypsy hadn't appealed to me very much, but I grew to feel very proud in deed.

What Hitler did to the Jews in World War II, he also did to the gypsies. He killed thousands of them; his intention as everyone knows was to bring Germany back to purebred stock. If he had wanted purebred Germans so badly, there was many ways he could have encouraged this without the killing of thousands of human beings. The man was either pure evil or just plain mad. On reflection, I'd say he was most probably, definitely both. And while we can't lay any blame on the following generations, it must never be allowed to be forgotten.

Romany Travellers are a breed unto themselves, and like any other people, there are the rich and there are the poor. The former would have beautifully kept caravans, decked out with brass and copper fixings; inside would have mirrors, pure china and exquisite lace and furnishings. They would trade in gold and horses, and take great care of their animals. But rich or poor alike, there was a set of rules to live by and being as one with nature, morals and hygiene applied to all.

If a Romany woman were unfaithful, she would be treated very harshly and shunned by all. In all honesty, I can't say the same for the men, but generally speaking families would have a very strong bond. Although our family tree proved to have lived in houses for quite a few generations, we still had relatives living in caravans. Dad took me a couple of times to introduce me to them. I think he needed to show me exactly how they lived and conducted themselves. I must say I was very impressed. This group had changed from horses to vehicles and their caravans were a sight to behold. Henceforth my idea of ever being embarrassed at being a gypsy was washed away forever.

Every family tree must have a few skeletons in the cupboard, and mine is no different. Dad was born in 1908, and in his late teens, his Uncle Sid would take him poaching for rabbits. There would be the nets, the ferrets and the dog, a Jack Russell, and they would set off late at night. They would locate a warren, block all the exits bar two, and the ferrets would be sent down. The dog would be waiting to pounce in case a rabbit was to break through. These rabbiting dogs would be very well trained, as well as being a family pet. A successful night would be a good catch, with no interruptions from the farmer's keepers. However, there was one occasion whilst on one of these excursions that they were indeed interrupted by not one, but four keepers. Dad and his Uncle Sid grabbed the nets up, and proceeded to shift themselves as fast as they could. To be caught would have meant a court appearance. The keepers were hot on their trail and Dad always claimed that they would have made it, if it hadn't been for the dog.

It thought its master was in trouble, and suddenly did a U-turn standing it's ground, and ready to take on all four keepers. Dad kept going until he heard his dog yelp.
He threw the nets to Uncle Sid and told him to run. They could not afford to have the nets confiscated; they cost too much money, so Uncle ran. Dad ran towards his dog in time to see it kicked again. He saw red, and waded in. He was eventually over powered, and at a later date did appear in court accused of poaching and grievous bodily harm. The four keepers arrived in the courtroom with different parts of their anatomy dressed in bandages. The judge stated, "I can't believe that this was all done by the accused. If I had more time I would order the bandages removed to confirm these injuries". He found it unbelievable that one man had done so much damage. Dad told the judge that he did indeed wade into them, but to protect his dog after they had kicked it twice. The judge dismissed

the bodily harm, and fined Dad for poaching. In the local Observer, the heading read, "Ruckus in Paddock Wood". The year was approximately 1930.

On another occasion, Dad and Uncle Sid were making their way through the woods and stumbled upon a man hanging from a tree. At a later date, it was realized he had in fact hung himself. But imagine finding something like that, two o'clock in the morning, the eerie silence, and barely able to see.

"We'd better report it Sid," Dad said. "It might even be someone local".

"No it's not," said Uncle Sid. "He was there last week and I went through his pockets. The silly bastard hadn't left any identification on himself, so let it be. Someone will find him. Can't help the silly bugger now".

Uncle Sid had fought in World War I and had seen front line action; a dead body wasn't anything new to him. He had seen so much death; there was an occasion when he jumped into a dug out to find a German there. He shot him, and then shot himself – in the kneecap. There were many men he said, that did inflict wounds upon themselves because they couldn't take any more. Battle fatigue wasn't recognized then as anything that needed medical treatment. I remember great Uncle Sid, but only as an old man, when he died I know my Dad felt quite deeply about his going, and would enjoy talking to me of some of his exploits. There were a couple of things he felt he couldn't tell me when Uncle was alive, but would be able to now he had past on. Dad proceeded to tell me of the time when Uncle Sid chased his woman out of the house, and down their street firing gun pellets at her rear end. She had done him wrong, with his voice ringing in her ears, telling her "don't ever come back or I'll finish the job".

A story he was to tell to Dad, asking he was never to breathe a word to a living soul, terrified him. Not for himself, but for Uncle Sid and while uncle was alive, Dad kept his word. Apparently on leaving the woods on one of his poaching trips, he walked straight into the arms of a copper. Uncle struggled to escape, but this copper was adamant he was going to get his man. A pretty heavy fight ensued, and uncle landed an almighty punch that sent the copper sprawling and he went down very heavily. Uncle stood breathing heavily and waited for the guy to get up, but he never moved. It didn't take many minutes for him to realize the cop was dead. Uncle told father there was no way that they were going to hang him.

So Dad asked him, "What did you do then?" His answer was very direct.

"I buried him".

My youngest brother seems to remember it somewhat differently. His memory of the incident was that Uncle Sid shot and killed a policeman while in a wood shooting birds for the dinner table, and served eight years in prison as a result, and was listed as an accident. Maybe these two incidents were completely unrelated.

In the process of stories being handed down, the circumstances surrounding the event can become distorted but one fact is clear, Great Uncle Sid did indeed kill a policeman.

Dad, as a teenager was apparently banned from the old part of Hastings for fighting. When he would speak of these years, I definitely got the impression that he was probably quite a handful for his Mother to deal with. I think it was her death that brought him to his senses. He felt the loss very deeply.

By the time he met Mother and fell in love, he was ready for the responsibility of bringing children into the world, and all that would entail. He had been previously married quite young, but it did not work out, and when Dad met Mum he asked for a divorce, but she repeatedly refused to grant him his freedom. On the death of his wife, Mum and Dad did indeed get married but it was all kept very hush hush. We were never to know until two years prior to Mum's death that us kids had all been born out of wedlock. By this time we were all married with youngsters of our own. Mum was so distressed when telling us. In her day, it would not have been acceptable and we would have been labelled 'bastards'. She said to the youngest of us, which was of course Chrissy, "At least you my darling were born in wedlock".

Mum had just given us our birth certificates, and as Chrissy read hers, she slowly shook her head and told Mum, "I'm a bastard too". Which brought on another flood of tears.

We assured Mum that it didn't bother us at all, and that we were content to keep it quiet if it made her happy.

My certificate stated I was born on the 29th July 1933, but all my life I had celebrated it on the 22nd, so I ended up with two birthdays. Mum claimed until her death, that the authorities were wrong. I changed all my legal documents to agree with my birth certificate for obvious reasons, but I still have my birthday celebrations on the 22nd. My sisters agreed, if the Queen could have two birthdays, why indeed not I.

Photograph of Mum and Dad, taken on one of Dads rare visits during world war two.

CHAPTER ELEVEN

Hastings Carnival 1952

I was seventeen and working as a waitress when a work mate and friend, a pretty girl with blonde wavy hair named Sheila, reminded me that it was the last day for entries for anyone wishing to enter The Hastings Carnival Queen Competition.

She suggested we went along in our lunch hour and put our names forward by signing the necessary forms. I told her I couldn't because I felt my Dad wouldn't like it, but that she should go ahead. So off she went. On her return she calmly informed me she had filled a form out for me. "Just ask your Dad and see what he says," she told me. So having convinced myself that nothing ventured, nothing gained, I approached Dad that same day after work, and was completely thrown when he said it was okay, but that brother John would go with me. He even bought me a lemon two-piece, and with my dark hair and a light summer tan, I felt very good. There were over fifty entries and we were lined up and then told to walk towards the table where three judges were sitting. They would speak to each girl in turn, asking two or three questions of each. When my turn came, I opened my mouth to answer, but no sound came out. I was so nervous my legs were wobbling. I thought there and then I'd blown it, but to my surprise I was amongst the ten that were selected to go on to the next stage. It must have been the lemon suit, along with my smile that saved me. It certainly wasn't anything I had said.

The next stage was evening dress, and was to be held at the White Rock Theatre a week later. The purpose was to select five of the ten that got through the first stage; one of which would be selected Queen, with the other four being Maids of Honour.

I went shopping and found a lovely simple dress with a halter neck. The colour was white, but I hadn't got enough money, so I paid a deposit and went to find my brother John. I explained to him that I couldn't possibly go to Dad again. My darling brother hadn't been working long, but said that if I would wait until payday, he would give me the amount I was short, which if I remember rightly was most of the total cost. I collected the dress the next day, Saturday. The competition was that evening, so it was all rather hectic.

Five girls were selected from the ten, and the lucky five were interviewed again to select the Queen. On that evening the crowd was definitely with me, and gave their support by stamping their feet and calling out to the judges. After an exchange of light conversation, the microphone was handed to me to address the crowd. You could have heard a pin drop. I think their enthusiasm gave me courage, my voice carried out crisp and clear. I thanked the judges, I thanked the organizers, and I thanked the audience for being there and for their support. It seemed a long time, but it was only a fifteen-minute wait. We were called back in and we waited with bated breath for the judges' decision.

I had won! The other girls were very gracious; they hugged and congratulated me while the crowd cheered, clapped and whistled. When you're seventeen, this is all rather exciting.

The date was June 1952; one month prior to my eighteenth birthday, and I was about to be crowned Queen for a week by Denis Day, who was an international singing star. He was very charming and took great pains not to mess up my hair when placing the crown upon my head. The dresses we were wearing were in the Elizabethan style. I don't know if they were the real thing or copies, but I was told they were insured for one thousand pounds. In 1952 that was quite a lot of money. 1953 was the coronation year of Queen Elizabeth II, which explains the choice, that the Carnival Committee had decided on. The dresses and ruffles around the neck were somewhat uncomfortable, but very appreciated by the public, especially the children.

Our chaperone had to teach us how to sit down; she did this by instructing us to do just that. This caused much laughter as the hoops stitched into the fabric stood up, revealing all the lower part of our bodies. It was imperative that we remembered to hitch up our skirts. During the whole of the week not one of us slipped up, I'm happy to say.

Coach and horses were to be our source of transport. There was a lot of waving and smiling. By the end of the week my face muscles were really aching. On Saturday 5th June following the crowning ceremony, I was escorted by the Mayor Alderman H.E. Rymill to inspect the Guard of Honour formed by the Hastings Sea Cadets.

There followed a wonderful and very enjoyable week and I was to meet many important people of the town including visiting dignitaries. It was to be a week of much celebration with a strong element of collecting as much money for charity as we could. Always very present was a group of people called The Revellers and they did a grand job dancing and clowning around whilst rattling their collection boxes. They were a credit to the town, and I believe it was a record week for collections that year. Also during the week was the National Town Crier's Championship for the News of the World Cup and replica. These people had the most powerful voices that you are ever likely to hear anywhere, and they performed for the judges and the public with great pride and gusto.

On Wednesday there was to be a fancy dress competition for children. This proved to be the most enjoyable day of that week for me, but it also proved to be the one and only time that I pleaded with the organizers to be excused. They had appointed me judge and it was the most impossible task they had asked of me. They were very understanding and quickly found someone else. I was very happy to sit on a very majestic throne that had been placed on a wooden boxed platform, with the children passing by me; some so young they were escorted by a parent, all dressed up in a wide variety of fancy costumes. They all looked so beautiful, but the thing that stands out in my mind is the expression on each of their little faces, as they looked up at me as they passed by one by one. On reflection I must have looked like someone straight out of a storybook - the throne, the very impressive crown on my head and the colourful costume of red and gold in the style of Queen Elizabeth I.

There must have been thousands of photographs taken that week, but I doubt if any were taken that would show the look of awe on the faces of those children.

It can still choke me up whenever my mind wonders back to that day. I also wonder who they are, where they are and what became of them, because now at this time of writing they would be in their fifties.

Came the last day of the week, Saturday 12th July, when the Carnival Possession was to take place. It was a lovely day; the sun shining, there was music everywhere and everybody was in such high spirits. The Revellers were out in force wearing colourful costumes and rattling their collection boxes. In 1952 Hastings, along with Hastings Old Town, was united and together they put on a large exciting procession. At some time along the way these two committees were to indulge in some kind of dispute, and up until this very day they still hold separate carnival celebrations.

The old part of Hastings, which was known for its own fishing fleet, would celebrate yearly and would call out for 'Winkles Up' by all its members. They would respond with much mirth, raising hands in the air that held specially designed winkle shells. Many visiting dignitaries would be called upon to 'Winkles Up' including Prince Phillip himself, whilst on a visit to Hastings. Sadly for the fishing fleet, the future was to hold many problems such as the Cod War and EUC political changes that were to control where the fishermen could fish. Whilst there still is a small fleet, I believe it has become exceedingly difficult for the men to earn a healthy living, and in my humble opinion runs the risk of eventually becoming none existent. That would be a very sad loss of a way of life for the Old Town Fishermen.

Anne Shelton, a singer of great repute, was performing that week at the Regal Theatre, and the girls and I were taken along to be introduced. She was blonde, attractive, with a figure of generous proportion, with a good strong voice that would fall very pleasantly on the ear. She had a very professional air about her and greeted me with a handshake and warm smile. So now with the week behind me and having received a small cash voucher to be spent at Plummers Store (which is now Debenhams), I was asked if there was anything on the lines of a gift that I would like to receive from the Carnival Committee for a job well done. I had no hesitation at all in asking for a large framed picture of myself in all my Elizabethan finery. I wanted it for Mum and Dad. They had already called into the shop where it was on display in the hope of purchasing it, but were told quite firmly that it was not for sale. They were very disappointed. So imagine my pleasure when it was handed to me with sincere thanks for all the efforts I had put into the week's events. We all said our good-byes with much hugging and kissing and the girls and myself were in agreement that it had indeed been a brilliant week. I was taxied home along with my picture and proudly presented it to Mum and Dad, who were obviously delighted.

There was much fan mail, but Dad being Dad, proclaimed he was not prepared for me to read most of it. With us girls he was inclined to be very protective, but he ordained to pass on one or two to me. One of which proclaimed me a ship's mascot, and I was able to send a photograph of myself, which had been placed in the News of the World. I was wearing a modest sun suit sitting on a large rock on the Hastings shoreline. Dad being an ex Marine must have decided these sailors were too far away to serve as any kind of threat.

I would mention at this point that Mary was voted Maid of Honour three years running, and Chrissy encouraged by Mary and I entered just the one time and was also voted Maid of Honour.
Quite an achievement for one family. I confess it to be a bit of a mystery that Dad allowed us this bit of harmless fun, but perhaps that is exactly how he viewed it himself.

Dennis Day, the international singing star,
crowning the 1952 Carnival Queen, Rebecca Bilsby.

12 Daily Graphic, July 7, 1952

HASTINGS QUEEN SHE CONQUERS IN CARNIVAL BEAUTY BATTLE

Carnival Queen Rebecca Bilsby inspects
the sea cadets with the Mayor, Alderman Rymill.
Rebecca wore a colourful robe for the ceremony.

A photo of me during my year as carnival queen

CHAPTER TWELVE

Dad and the Boys

When Dad first started up in the Scrap Metal business, his billheads would show 'A.H Bilsby & Sons'. My brothers were very young and still had quite a few years to go before they could be of any help to Dad. But, even in their early teens, Dad would get them to earn their pocket money by collecting scrap wood and making neat bundles that they secured with elastic bands and sold around the local area for firewood. They did very well for themselves because apart from the cost of elastic bands, which were very cheap, they had no other financial outlay. In those early years Dad like Mum worked very hard to keep us all well fed and clothed. It couldn't have been easy; he started off with just a little brown second-hand van and would go out daily buying and collecting scrap. He would advertise for people to bring their old vehicles to the yard, and depending on the condition of the said vehicle would agree a price. He would dismantle these vehicles, and customers would be able to buy spare parts including tyres, that still offered some good tread. Dad became so busy that he offered a cheaper price if customers were to dismantle the required part themselves. Sunday mornings would find Dad sitting in his office, while the yard would be full of men tinkering about with screwdrivers, pliers, even hammers, and getting great pleasure out of saving themselves a few bob. Dad would come up to the house, clean himself up and set off to his local pub for his usual couple of pints of brown ale, which he claimed gave him a great appetite for Mum's Sunday lunch. Pubs would have lunchtime sessions and evening sessions, and the law was very strict. Landlords wanted no trouble with the local bobby on the beat.

Eventually Dad was to buy a second-hand lorry, which would enable him to transport large loads of scrap metal. So the business was to continue in this vein until the boys; one by one left school and worked for Dad earning a wage. As they grew into young men everything would be going on well including working together in the yard, and their social activities at the weekends. The boys would be out on the town after the hard weeks work routine; they'd earned it. Dad always joined the boys on these occasions, and soon became accepted as being one of the lads. This relationship was to continue on and off all his life. It was your typical "One for all and all for one" – The Four Musketeers.

As time went on, Dad and the boys were to have quite fiery disputes over the business, but they always managed to resolve these problems and put it all behind them. Mum was always happy to see them go out together, safety in numbers she would say, and if the truth were known she was very happy indulging in her quiet game of bingo.

Whilst Dad and the boys never went out looking for trouble, it would often find them, but local boys soon realized it was best to leave the 'Bilsby Boys' alone. Dad would say to me that there were three types of behaviour whilst under the influence of alcohol: those that were to sleep, those that wanted to sing and dance, and those that just wanted to fight. In between their fiery disputes there would be hilarious times too.

Dad purchased some scrapped buses from Eastbourne that had to be driven back to Hastings to the scrap yard and be dismantled. It proved to be quite a task. Under today's law they would not have been allowed to do that; the buses were considered to be no longer road worthy. They would drive over to Eastbourne in the lorry and three would drive buses back. On one occasion, Dad was in the front bus, John in the third and Robert in the middle bus. When Dad saw Robert overtaking him waving his arms about in the air, he thought something was wrong; "What the fuck did the boy think he was doing?" Dad was later to find out that Robert had no brakes. I don't know how he got the bus under control! I think he must have stopped half way up a hill. The journey was completed by Robert's bus being towed by the lorry. With the brakes being non-functional, Robert had controlled the bus by using the handbrake.

On another occasion, again driving three buses back with John in the rear bus, they were warned that John's bus had a very difficult gearbox. It was claimed that they had found only one bus driver who could drive it, even whilst rolling a cigarette with one hand. Dad and Robert arrived back at the yard and got back to work, occasionally looking at the clock and wondering what was holding John up. Two hours later he did arrive and he was asked, "where the fuck have you been?" and "what took you so long?" The poor guy had driven the bus all the way in first gear; he was not a happy boy. John would, on occasion disappear to the yard loo with the 'Exchange and Mart' tucked under his arm: a magazine advertising the selling and buying of various vehicles. It was the only place he said that he could find a bit of peace and quiet.

Dad would often close the yard down and take us all hop picking, cherry picking or sometimes apple picking. Not only was it a good source of money for the family, but also it was a way of life that I think Dad had some difficulty in letting go of. He really enjoyed, as we all did, the outside life style. This would continue, even when we were all married and had young children to consider, so we generally joined this little band if it was in the school holidays and partners were in agreement. But, as the children grew older it became increasingly more difficult, and it was to gradually fade away and become a thing of the past. But we would often reflect on these times, especially the more humorous aspect of events. Dad once agreed a price with a farmer and bought the cherries still on the trees. This is a brave decision to take because Dad and the farmer together would decide how much fruit grew on the trees, what the current price would be, and of course there was the unpredictable weather to be considered; not forgetting the birds that ate great quantities prior and during the picking season, which would last approximately three weeks. There was one particular great big tree that held a great abundance of cherries, but the farmer informed Dad that the tree was rotten right through and strongly advised him to forget about harvesting the fruit. So the task of protecting the fruit from the birds was set out a couple of weeks before picking was to commence. Two of the boys would arrive in the Orchard and along with the farmer set up three or four contraptions that would periodically go off with an almighty bang and it was strongly recommended that you kept your distance, as the noise could temporarily affect your hearing. These preset contraptions could not be used on a twenty four-hour basis out of consideration for people who lived nearby. So my two brothers would be up and about at three thirty every morning walking around the Orchard brandishing wooden rattlers in an attempt to scare the birds away from the fruit. Once the Cherries were considered to be ready for picking, we would all arrive at the farm, brush out the huts, and make up the beds on bales of straw that had been supplied by the farmer.

Dad would dig out a large hole some distance from the huts, and surround it with a wooden structure that would serve as a loo. Then on the day we left, Dad would fill the hole in, thereby leaving the landscape as we had found it. With the campfire now well on the way, Mum would prepare and cook a main meal, then it was early to bed. Dad would ask for two volunteers for the next day's early morning task of getting up with the birds in order to protect his financial investment. Everyone was to take their turn at this job, and I must say there was something quite enjoyable about walking through the Orchard at quarter to four in the morning with no sound other than the twittering of birds and a fresh gentle breeze to slowly bring your senses back to full awareness. It was one of these occasions of being half asleep and half awake at about three o'clock in the morning that Mum made a sleepy dash to the loo, having hoisted her nightie up and proceeded to 'spend a penny', when her son John said, "Mum, what do you think your doing?" She screamed with fright whilst jumping almost out of her skin. Dad came rushing out thinking someone was being murdered (at the least). Mum claimed the experience would probably stay with her for the rest of her life, not to mention the embarrassment of bearing her bum to her son. John tried to reassure her that he hadn't seen anything, as it was too dark. Then it was time for Dad to check the fruit and decide which trees were to be harvested first. The cherries were weighed and boxed and then collected on a daily basis, usually late afternoon by contracted distributors. Towards the end of the harvesting, Dad was happy to announce that we had done well and we would receive our just rewards. Even the weather had been just right for the cherry season.

Well, as for the large rotting tree that was left alone on the farmer's note, Dad was to find the boys under it gazing up and declaring, "It's almost criminal to leave such an abundance of fruit to rot". They managed to convince Dad that if they placed two ladders on opposite sides of the tree, thereby supporting each other's weight, they could carefully and slowly harvest this fruit. Dad finally agreed but made the boys promise that the first sign of anything untoward, they would drop their baskets and just jump clear. So, cousin Harry and Jim both in unison placed their ladders and very carefully ascended this great tree and commenced picking. Everything was fine until Aunt Rose; a visiting relative, unaware of the danger pending was kindly collecting wood to keep the open fire going so Dad wouldn't have to relight it. She was aimlessly wandering when she came upon a large piece of wood and placed it up against the tree the boys were harvesting. They were so quiet, not talking, singing or whistling (as was the norm), but just picking and listening for the slightest warning of danger. Well, Auntie gave this piece of wood one almighty whack with her foot to break it in two. Both cousin Harry and Jim let their baskets of cherries drop and both jumped off the top of their ladders and rolled across the ground and sprung to their feet expecting to see the tree fall, and trying to decide which way they should run. But instead they were staring at Auntie Rose with their mouths wide open. Everyone was running towards the scene fearing fractured limbs at least, but nobody had been hurt at all. Auntie was later to state that it was the first time her son Harry; who was aged about thirty had ever sworn at her in the whole of his life and claimed she would never be able to forget that fact. So much for the memory of the havoc she had caused, just by collecting pieces of firewood. The boys, who were never known to say die, climbed back up the tree with Dad now on guard and were to successfully finish what they had started. The next year was to show that the farmer had cut down the said tree, to the disappointment of the boys. They claimed they had been looking forward to repeating the challenge.

In the wintertime, Dad and the boys managed to build up a wood round. They would buy lorry loads of logs and axe them down to sizeable pieces, bag them and sell to local people for their winter fires. On one occasion, when some wooded land had been thinned out Dad would offer a price and hire a sawmill and cut and bag on the spot. This proved to be a very good earner. As time went on and all three boys were married, disputes over the business were to become intolerable for everyone. Brother Jim being the quietest one of the three decided he'd had enough and took a job on a building site where he claimed he could earn more money. John and Robert put it to Dad that they were no longer prepared to work as hard as they did for anything less than a partnership, but had no wish to deprive Dad from remaining at the helm. Reluctantly Dad was to agree and for a few years this was to prove to be successful. Then the boys asked Dad to join them in purchasing a press, this would enable them to shift scrap cars at a much faster rate. This venture would take what capital they had, and Dad was doubtful. But the boys eventually convinced him they could make it pay and make it pay well. As time went on the press was to prove itself worthy of the huge financial investment. Not only did it earn its worth, but also proved to be a very comfortable income for all concerned.

Dad finally reached the stage of his life where he needed some diversity from the yard, so he bought for himself a little workman's café. It was situated on a corner off Norman Road, and so of course it was called "The Corner Café". The boys didn't see too much of him for about a week while he familiarized himself with the general idea of being a café proprietor, with a staff of three; a cook, general cleaner and washer up, and lastly a young woman to wait tables. At some point when the cook needed to be replaced, Dad talked Mum into taking the job over. Business was to boom; Mum was a very good cook. Well, she had certainly had enough practice at it, but two years on her health was to suffer; quite possibly due to the steam created in the kitchen. I spoke to father and suggested that the time had come for him to now replace Mother. He claimed once she was made well, she would be perfectly okay to return to the kitchen. Mum was fast approaching the age of fifty and was developing a bronchial condition. She was the youngest of twenty-two children, and claimed that she had always felt that there was a slight weakness in her lungs, and wasn't at all surprised that it had finally caught up with her. Three weeks later, I was to find her back in the kitchen; but within three days that she had been back, she was again looking and feeling unwell. I told her that she must talk to Dad, and get herself away from the kitchen. She claimed that she would do so. The next day when I checked in on her, she looked terrible. "No," she said, "I haven't spoken to your father". So I waited until lunch was over, and I took her home and put her to bed. "I don't want to let your Dad down my darling," she said to me. I told her that I would talk to Dad myself. So having phoned the doctor for a repeat prescription for antibiotics, I left and went in search of Dad. It was one of a very few occasions that Dad and I were to have words. He claimed I was interfering with something that was none of my concern. I, in turn, accused him of not only being blind but also selfish, and I told him that he should go home and really look at Mother with both eyes open. The doctor made a visit that evening and spoke to father. Mum never returned to the steamy kitchen, and Dad was able to resolve his staff problem, and neither Dad nor I ever brought the subject up again. As always in our family, disputes were soon forgotten. Mum was to enjoy a well-earned retirement, apart from looking after Dads needs and keeping her little home as always, spick and span.

This was to leave her plenty of time to enjoy grandchildren that had made their presence felt by this time in her life, and what a wonderful and loving grand Mother she made. She never forgot her favourite game of Bingo.

Misfortune was to fall on the business in the shape of a letter from the local council, informing Dad that there was to be, in the not too distant future, a compulsory purchase notice set upon the premises. Thereby, putting Dad and the boys out of business. The yard, the lock ups, and the surrounding area that housed many people (including us), were to be torn down and rebuilt upon. A year later, by which time we were all married, Mum and Dad were re-housed in a very nice two-bedroom house in Firle Close, Downs Farm, Fairlight. Dad still had the café, so it left the boys, including Jim, to set up a business on their own.

John bought a small garage and slowly built up a trade repairing vehicles. Jim, with his small truck, bought and sold metals and would turn his hand to all sorts of jobs, and managed to earn a decent living. Robert bought skip lorries, bought and sold second-hand cars, and also dealt in metals. So, it appeared all had managed to survive. The press that had served them so well was sold and brought a very good price. An era had come to an end, but there is only one way to go and that's forward. The boys have always been and still are their own boss.

Dad taught them many things, and how to earn a good living has to be somewhere at the top of a very long list.

CHAPTER THIRTEEN

Love and Marriage

Having taken time out since writing about Hastings Carnival, in order to write about Dad and the Boys, I will now continue my story by telling you that following the end of the wonderful week I had as Carnival Queen, I was to be given a party for my eighteenth birthday and with invitations sent out to family and friends I continued setting out to work daily with an inner excitement building up inside me. At that time one's eighteenth was not a special birthday. Coming of age then was twenty-one, so I felt this special party was partly to do with my most recent success of Queen for a week. Unbeknown to me at this time was the arrival of a young man in a Royal Air Force uniform knocking on the door and asking Dad if he minded taking in his case and kit bag, as his Mother who lived in the flat across from us was out and he didn't as yet have a key. Dad invited him in for a cup of tea and they sat chatting. Dad was to learn that his name was Edward Blakeley and he had just completed his two-year conscript. He preferred to be called Ted, so when I arrived home, that's what Dad introduced him as.

Dad for reasons only known to himself had always called me Bett instead of Beck or Becky, which of course is short for Rebecca, and as Dad was the person to introduce me to Ted, he knew me as Bett.

After Ted had thanked us and said his good-byes, Dad was to tell me how he found this young man very much to his liking. A couple of days prior to my party, he suggested I go up to Ted and invite him; so I did, and I even gave him a lift there and back. As the party came to a close, I realised Ted had gone missing, so I went around this large flat in search of him and found him fast asleep stretched out in the bath tub. Little did I know then that this would be the start of love's journey down through the years for us both.

I wasn't to see Ted again for a couple of weeks, and during that time Mary and I was to be invited by two boys we knew to ride pillion on their new motorbikes. We were both aware that Dad having forbidden such past times would be extremely angry with us if he should find out. The boys coaxed us, saying if we didn't tell they wouldn't, and it would only be for a short spin. We both found the thrill of it all too much to say 'no'. So away we went, the wind blowing through our hair. Crash helmets were not compulsory then. I found it exciting. All would have been well if one of the bikes hadn't developed a small problem. One boy stayed with us and the bikes, and the other set off walking back to the nearest garage. It was an hour before he was to return, and then to find that the small pin was the wrong size. He proceeded to file it down by rubbing it down using the pavement. Mary and I were now really panicking. I remember this young man making his knuckles bleed to comply with our pleas to hurry. Once he got the bike mobile again they got us home as fast as they could in one piece, and if I remember rightly they were quite relieved to see the back of us. Dad was waiting for us. He looked so very stern.

As Dad was so adamant about motorbikes being off limits, Mary and I decided it best to omit telling about bikes, but just admit to spending time with these two boys and apologise for being late. But something was wrong; Dad was looking at us so very oddly.

"I will repeat the question," he said, "Where have you been?"
So, again we repeated our little white lie. At this point Dad slapped my purse on the table.

"A police woman just brought this to me and claimed it was found this side of Rye and handed in to the police station. They were concerned enough to bring it straight away and now I shall have to phone them and let them know you are both home and safe."
He told us we were grounded evenings for a week, and not as punishment for the motorbike ride, but for lying to him. We slunk off to the bedroom and breathed a sigh of relief and felt we had got off lightly.

I was coming home from work one evening and not looking forward to another night in when I bumped into Ted. We stopped and chatted and as we parted he asked me if I would like to go to the pictures. I said, "I'll have to ask my Dad," and that I would let him know.

I waited for Dad to wash up and eat his dinner and asked please would he let me off the hook for just one evening, as I'd been invited to go to the pictures. He was ages answering me.

"Is it that nice young man across from us," he asked.

"Yes," I replied.

"Don't be late back or you will pay by having another week's grounding."

"I won't Dad," I promised.

So that was my first date with Ted. He was to learn very early on in our relationship how strict Dad was with us girls, and he noted that Dad was not like it with my brothers. This gave me food for thought. It was possible to approach Dad with queries and questions, so I did. His answer to me left me no room for argument.

"The boys will grow up to be men, and need to experience all things. But you girls, whether you like it or not will grow up to be ladies," and I think it's true to say he more or less did achieve what he wanted to.

Dad would tell us that there was no such thing as perfection, but he could think of no reason why we should not strive towards it. To seek perfection in others could only bring us unhappiness. Speaking for myself, everyone is a nice person until they prove otherwise. The only way that Dad was to treat us all the same would be, if he gave sixpence to one; he gave to all of us, and discipline was always just. Also, boys and girls alike were taught to be streetwise and to defend themselves.

My brothers were members of a young boys boxing club. John my eldest brother did extremely well and competed with other clubs, but at some point Dad stopped it all. He wasn't keen for John to follow this profession big time. His intention had been only to toughen them up and this he had achieved to his satisfaction. Also at this stage in my life, I had four girl friends; June, Beryl, Sheila and one late arrival to the scene, and I am sad to say that I am unable to recollect her name. The five of us were nicknamed 'The Five Rosebuds'. We were always together, and we met up in a favourite coffee shop in Hastings Town Centre, from where we would swan around the town; pretty much what young people do today. I'm probably repeating myself, but there was nothing like the violence and vandalism that is to be found today back then, even amongst the very young; it saddens me greatly.

My second date with Ted proved just a little bit disastrous. It was a Sunday morning, and I wanted to take him along to the café and introduce him to the girls. Well, I think it proved all too much for him to cope with; he spilt his coffee. I quickly said my good-byes and ushered Ted out of there, and did not attempt to repeat the experience again. From that point on, I did keep in touch with the girls but my time was spent with Ted. Eventually the girls were to spread their wings and move away chasing their own dreams, and eventually we lost touch altogether.

As our relationship developed, Ted was to make it quite clear he had no interest in dancing, and as I loved dancing, I realize now I must have had very strong feelings for him to so easily comply with his wishes. We had been dating about three months when Dad informed me that we were all once again taking off to the hops fields and as that meant I would be away for at least five to six weeks. I did complain to Dad. Although I was eighteen, he was adamant about not leaving me behind to fend for myself. He claimed it would be a test for Ted and myself regarding our growing affection for each other. So, I said my good-byes to Ted and once again the family set out for the hop gardens. I was surprised to find myself missing Ted, even though we had only dated about three months, so six weeks I felt was going to seem a long, long time. We wrote to each other, and eventually Dad was called home to tend to the yard on about the fourth Saturday. So once the Saturday shopping was done and the trip to Tenterden was over, Dad set off for home and was to return to us that same evening. Dad was not famous for taking U-turns, but on this occasion he had. He had brought back a surprise for me; someone he thought I might like to see. Ted slipped out of Dad's vehicle and appeared from around the back and presented himself to me. It was so unexpected that I couldn't help but show my pleasure. He just stood there grinning at me.

After we had eaten the evening meal, I walked around the campfire and thanked Dad with a kiss on his cheek.

"I should think so," he said "I have to repeat the trip tomorrow to take Ted home"

Ted had to go to work on the Monday.

On the evening of his arrival, and after I helped with the clearing up, Ted and I went for a walk around the hop gardens, just chatting about nothing much in particular. We eventually found ourselves in the middle of a hop garden that had been picked clean of its growth of hops. All that was left was a field full of wooden poles that had been sunk into the ground and served as a climbing frame for the young vines that had been planted at each base. It was at one of these poles that Ted was to stop me, take me into his arms and kiss me. This of course I was waiting for and was expecting. But what really took me completely by surprise was when he quietly asked me to marry him. My immediate answer was 'yes', and that was the second surprise I experienced that evening. He certainly had picked the right moment. It was a lovely warm early September evening; the moon was out and ready to play its part in the romance, and the kiss that was to seal the pledge we made to each other. Everyone was excited about our news, but Dad was to make it quite clear there would be no marriage until I reached the age of twenty-one.

Ted was working for British Railways and hoping for promotion, which would enable him to become a guard on the main line network. I had acquired a job as waitress in a seafront hotel called the Medlow.

In his break time he would come along and chat with me through the open window. We would meet up every evening and sometimes go to the pictures. Ted was saving as much as he could to buy me an engagement ring and I was saving towards my 'bottom draw'.

Christmas was three months away and we both decided this would be a lovely time to get engaged. Life was to amble on happily for us both, and we were growing ever closer as the weeks wore on. I was to realise that Ted had a very strong tendency to be quite jealous, but fortunately neither of us were flirtatious so it did not cause too much of a problem. A few days before Christmas Ted was to lead me into a jewellery shop and told me how much he had saved and I was to look at some rings. I felt really excited. The assistant brought out trays of various designs for me to look at and try on. Suddenly there it was, a very dainty pretty ring: a ruby stone with a small diamond on each side of it. I asked to try it on and it fitted perfectly. It had been made, I felt, just for me. Ted asked the assistant the price and I just held my breath waiting with the word 'please!' running around in my head. The next thing I knew, the assistant was putting the ring in a box and then into a small bag. A small family gathering on Christmas Eve, and Ted placed the ring on my finger. We were both so very happy. Months went by, and Mother looked at me one day and said, "You are losing too much weight". She promptly took me round to the doctors for a check up. Tests were taken, and nothing could be found to be wrong with me. Dr Ingham told Mother to bring me back the following week, which she did, and it was found that I had lost yet another two pounds in weight. More tests were taken, with the same results, and still I continued to lose weight steadily. Eight and a half stone reduced now to just over seven stone. Everyone was now getting worried including myself. It was indeed a mystery as I was eating, and Ted would take me to café's and buy me suppers. Mother was feeding me with choice bits and spoonfuls of malt, and still the weight was slipping off. Dr Ingham marched me down to the room of his senior partner, Dr Gabb, and proclaimed he was at a loss, as he couldn't find anything wrong with me. Dr Gabb was what I would call a military man and very out spoken indeed, and although I was now the age of nineteen, he was to embarrass me unforgettably. He leaned across his desk, looked me straight in the eye and asked:

"Are you courting?"

"Yes," I replied, sincerely.

"Are you having sex?"

"No," I whispered.

"When are you getting married?"

I told him that Dad had said I must wait until I'm twenty-one.

"You tell you're father there won't be anything left of you if you do that. If it's necessary, send your father round to see me."

I left his room and my face must have been as red as beetroot. I told Mum, and together we put Dad in the picture. I think Dad was only too happy to comply to an earlier wedding, as he was so relieved that there was nothing seriously wrong with me.

I had been fretting the weight off. To have sex before marriage in my day was not the done thing. Well, not by a well brought up young lady.

So, a Christmas wedding was planned, instead of the summer wedding in July of the following year. Mother had said that everyone would think her daughter was pregnant because the wedding was being brought forward.

I teasingly dared to stuff a cushion up my jumper, but it was obvious by the blank expressions on my parent's faces that they were not amused. But time itself was to dispel any queries in that department as it was well over a year before I gave birth to my first son.

Dad promised to do the best he could for us regarding a Wedding Reception. Ted and I continued to save as much as we could for our important day. When I discovered how expensive wedding dresses were, I decided to answer ads that were offering wedding dresses at very reasonable prices. It didn't take me very long to find one that fitted me perfectly and I felt very pleased with myself for I had saved quite a lot of money. We would walk the streets looking for flats to let, and felt very lucky when we found one that was being renovated and would come available about three weeks prior to our wedding date. No deposit or rent was required until that time, so again we were saving costs. We both decided it would be a good idea to make weekly payments on a bedroom suite and this we did religiously. By the time we were married, the suite would be paid in full.

Well laid plans we thought; but we were in for a double shock. The wedding was now only five weeks away and upon arriving to pay the deposit of one month's rent in advance, we were sadly informed that "the powers that be" had failed the newly renovated flat on several points, and declared it unfit for letting. She offered us a room and use of kitchen in her guesthouse until such time as we were able to find other accommodation. We felt we had little choice and so accepted her offer. One week prior to the wedding, I was to receive a letter from a furniture store, that they had been declared Bankrupt, so we lost our lovely bedroom suite.

Not to be daunted, the wedding plans continued, and the date set for December 31st, 1953. We met and chatted to our local vicar, and I surprised him by claiming a preference to be married in the little old church rather than the big new church on the sea front. I think I made his day, and for three weeks the banns were read announcing our forthcoming marriage. Then came the big day, everything seemed to come together even the weather was very kind; a little chilly, but then it was December. When you are one of a very large family, it's not often possible to get everyone together. It takes an important event, such as a Wedding to achieve this.

Dad, as promised, gave us a lovely evening reception, and a grand time was had by all.
Ted and I finally said our good byes to everyone with much hugging, kissing and some teasing, and made our way to the room at the Guesthouse. We promised each other that it would not be for long, and we would search for a flat and begin to build our home as soon as the holiday period was over.

Luck had not been totally on our side, but we were in love and were not to be daunted. It took three months to find a flat; it wasn't brilliant, but at least we could get away from that one room and start to build a home.

    'Mr. & Mrs. Blakeley
    No. 6 Stanhope Place, St Leonard's'

Me and Ted on our wedding day

Me and Ted in the early days of our marriage

Me and My Dad

It was damp and it was smelly but we worked at it, and as each piece of furniture was bought and placed, it gradually began to resemble a home. There were two more flats above us; making three in all, and we all shared the front door. So you had to lock the kitchen and both bedroom doors to feel secure. The back bedroom was so damp; mildew grew on the walls, so that room stayed permanently locked. This was no place to start a family so I placed our name on the Hastings Council Housing List. In due course a man arrived to assess the flat. He sympathised, but assessment was made on how much space we lived in, as opposed to the condition of the premises. He was at least very honest with us; the prospect of us getting a council flat was practically nil, even though the second bedroom was unusable.

The weight I had lost prior to my getting married was, to everyone's delight, putting back on, so we decided to go ahead with our plans to start a family whilst continuing to look for better accommodation. But we were to become very disillusioned. Flats were like gold dust, and seemed unobtainable by young couples, either with children or with couples planning to have children. We would read ads like "no children, no pets, and no bikes". Ted at the time had a pushbike that he used to get him to and from work and we were definitely planning a family so that left us out of the running.

Ted and I were to experience our first quarrel; what it was about I have failed to remember. But never the less we had planned to go to the pictures, and set out on our way to the Regal Cinema. It was but a ten-minute walk from home, and en-route Ted was muttering away at me so I proceeded to walk on ahead to avoid any further argument. This annoyed him and he grabbed my long hair and pulled me back and set me to walk behind him. I did see red, and I grabbed his shirt and ripped it off his back and ran all the way back home. I sat on the bed and waited for him to follow. What could be keeping him I thought to myself? I was to later find out. Mum and Dad lived nearby and Ted had decided to confront my father. I was to learn later that Ted had showed father what I had done and declared how could he possibly tame me when he had my father and three brothers to answer to. Dad informed him that as long as he didn't draw blood he had his blessing. He told Ted to go home and place me across his knee and spank my arse. I might state at this point that Ted never mentioned the fact that he had pulled me by the hair. Ted arrived home and did exactly that. He lifted up my skirt pulled down my knickers and gave me a sound spanking. It really hurt; my tears proved to be too much for him and ironically, we ended up making passionate love. All's well that ends well. Ted had taken the first steps in taming a high-spirited filly, and I had learnt one of the secret weapons that all females have over the man who loves her: tears.

After six months of married life I was still not pregnant, and decided to see my doctor. As Dr Ingham was on holiday, I found myself once again in the presence of Dr Gabb, whose outspoken attitude had so embarrassed me regarding my weight loss prior to my getting married. He said I was looking well, and asked what he could do to help me.

Upon telling him that I was unable to get pregnant and desperately wanting to have a baby, he enquired how long had I been trying, to which I replied "two months".

"Good God woman, I have couples on my books that have been trying for years"

He advised that when next Ted and I made love to follow it through by making love first thing in the morning. Because of Ted's shift work on the railways this had to be planned out. Well, why this advise worked I had no idea but, I became pregnant very quickly, and having counted the nine months off on my fingers realized I would be able to hold this precious bundle in my arms in April of the next year 1955. Once I was through the stage of early morning sickness and losing my usual healthy appetite, I found myself at four and a half months experiencing a very strong desire for ice cream, and I would consume bowls of the stuff. Ted would ask me every evening if I wanted any. There were a few occasions when I would decline. But usually, as the clock ticked away towards nine (which was the time that the local ice-cream parlour would close) I would look at him in a certain way, and he would grab a glass bowl and dash to the parlour. His compensation was the very attractive blonde who would be waiting poised with the ice-cream scoop at the ready.

Ted was obviously a source of amusement, but he wasn't to enlighten me of these facts for many years.

In my first year of married life I was to learn a lot about Ted's childhood. His Mother brought him over from Ireland when he was just six years old, and it took his father some time to track them down. Although Ted was at that time in a home for boys, and his Mother in the local workhouse, whilst constantly searching for a job and a place to live, this in itself was not enough grounds to enable his father to take him back to Ireland with him. The choice was eventually put to Ted himself and he chose to stay in England with his Mother. His father was left feeling very bitter towards his Mother, and Ted was not to see his father again for many years. Helen, Ted's Mother, was to find herself unemployed many times, and Ted would end up back in care. She was to meet a man and fall pregnant, but when she gave this man the news, he was to promptly disappear, and Helen eventually gave birth to a baby girl, who she named Margaret. Helen was to meet and live with a man named Adge, and they had two boys, Richard and Geoffrey. Unfortunately, Adge was also to up and leave. So life must have been very difficult for them all. Ted was preparing at the age of seventeen for his compulsory two-year conscription and was pleased that he was accepted into the Royal Air Force. He left behind his Mother, half sister and two half brothers (that were at that time reunited, and preparing to move into the flat opposite from my parent's home). Come April 1955, I was to give birth to our son Teddy. He was christened Edward Alfred Blakeley; Edward after his father, and Alfred after my father. A very healthy happy baby. Ted and I were in our element; this was a new life that together we had created. What greater gift could life bestow upon us?

When Teddy was distressed, especially when he started teething, I would place his cot alongside my bed, slip my hand through the cot bars and he would settle down to sleep gripping my forefinger tightly.
After a time and many sleepless nights Ted and I decided to introduce the dummy for sleeping times only. What a godsend that proved to be. It gave Teddy comfort and Ted and I blessed sleep. I

don't think back then or even now that young people are made fully aware of how demanding these small people can be, and their lungpower can be extremely ear piercing. It is a twenty four-hour job.

You find yourself sleeping with one eye and one ear on the alert, and quite often just waking up and quietly approaching the cot and listening intently for the sound of your baby's breathing. I drew comfort from the fact that I was a light sleeper and didn't seem to have much trouble getting back off to sleep. Sound advice from my son's grandparents was a great source of comfort to me especially in those early months. There was the weekly baby clinic, and when the nurse would tell me the baby was making great progress I would feel any anxiety that had built up over the past week, leave my mind and body, and leave me feeling really proud of myself.

As time went on I found myself becoming more and more relaxed and really enjoying Motherhood. Ted and I chose a pram that was really more than we could afford. It was a shiny jet black "Marmit" that had lots of silver chrome work, with two large and two small wheels. It really was a showpiece. I would clean and polish it until it gleamed, bath and dress Teddy, and he would lay in his pram smiling and cooing, then off I would stroll and proudly show him off to anyone who would care to stop and admire him. When Ted's shift work allowed him to, he would join me on these outings. I asked him once how it made him feel. He said it made him feel that his shoulders were ten feet wide. I always thought that that had said it all really. I was soon to discover what real anxiety was all about. Teddy became ill and showed to have a high temperature. The doctor was called; he tried to calm my fears and gave me some sound advice along with a prescription for medication that would help to bring down his temperature. He was just eight months old and I had never felt this scared. Ted and I spent the first night with hardly any sleep. I decided to move Teddy's cot down to the living room and a blanket for myself and I was to get what sleep I could in an armchair. Ted had to get his sleep if he was going to keep fit for work and as I was not working at this time I could catch catnaps during the day.

By the fourth day, Teddy's fever broke around two o'clock in the morning. He was still very poorly and I could not trust myself to sleep. Ted's Mum, Helen, arrived that morning and told us she would return in the evening and sit up all night with Teddy while I went to bed and got some badly needed sleep. "You look exhausted," she said to me. To my amazement I slept right through the night. I hadn't even heard Ted get up and go off to work. I dashed down to the living room and peered into the cot to be welcomed by the most wonderful sight of my baby smiling up at me.

As your child grows, so does your experience and confidence; which is just as well, because there were to be many such experiences in the process of bringing up my children.

Ted and I had not planned to have any more children until we had found better accommodation, but someone was in a hurry to be part of this loving trio. So it was with a mixture of concern and excitement that I gave Ted the news that I was pregnant.

"Don't worry," he said, "We will cope".

Bare in mind this flat of ours didn't even have a bathroom, only a back scullery that housed a cooker, a sink and of course the ever reliable tin bath. The living room measured only 11' x 8' but thankfully the bedroom being a generous 14' x 12' would be able to house two cots quite comfortably. It was during my second pregnancy that Ted's Mum Helen became very ill.

Ted informed me that she was not eating much at all, so I would take her round some tasty dishes but she couldn't be tempted. Ted was to phone for the doctor to make a house call, only to have her rushed by ambulance to our local hospital, where Helen was prepared for an immediate operation. The doctor informed Ted on his arrival at the hospital that there was nothing they could do for her. She was in such an advanced stage of cancer and he should prepare himself for the worst. I'm sad to say she never returned home and died in hospital within days. It is often said that a woman can be all things to the man in her life, and that night I held Ted as a Mother would hold and soothe her child. He cried for the loss of his Mother and the fact that he had had so little warning. It was almost as if one minute she was there, and the next she was gone. It would be days before he was able to talk about her.

She was somewhat eccentric and I firmly believe that so was her cat. They would go to the picture house together. Helen would wear her slippers for comfort, and she would select an end seat, and the cat would sit in the isle and would watch the performance through to the end, without so much as a twitch of its whiskers. A neighbour had come to Ted one day and told him how sorry he was that his Mum's cat had been found dead; it had been hit by a car. As Ted was on his way to work the neighbour kindly offered to take it to the vets for decent disposal, and Ted gave him seven shillings and sixpence to cover expenses. He quickly popped into his Mother to break the news, as he didn't want her to find out from anyone else. Helen and his sister, and the two brothers were very upset, but Ted finally left and made his way to his place of work. Helen had always wrapped a piece of cloth around the door knocker to stop the cat knocking them up in the small hours of the morning, but as the cat was now dead she removed the cloth, and everyone sadly took themselves off to bed. It was about two thirty in the morning when they were all woken up by the sound of the doorknocker banging away. The kids all jumped onto their Mum's bed screaming that the cat's ghost had come to haunt them. Helen calmed them down and very gingerly approached the door and slowly opened it, and her cat calmly walked in. It seems that Ted had paid seven shillings and sixpence to bury someone else's cat.

Helen's children were too young to be left to fend for themselves. Margaret was seventeen and working. Richard was almost fifteen and Geoffrey thirteen years of age and both still at school. When the social worker called on us, Ted and myself both stated positively that we could not see the boys go back into a care home and that we were prepared to give them a home with us. But we asked if their department would help us with a new application to the Hastings Council for a council house. I was now seven months pregnant with no desire for ice cream at all. Instead I was getting through a constant supply of lemonade - bottles and bottles of the stuff. The empties would be lined up in the back scullery waiting for Ted to take back to the shop to retrieve the three pence on each bottle returned.

The next two months were pretty hectic for all of us, so by the time my first pains started I was more than happy to find myself back in the maternity nursing home with my second child well and truly on the way. Ted was left to cope at home as best he could.

I felt a great heaviness in the lower part of my stomach and climbed upon the bed, then pressed the buzzer that would bring the nurse. She popped her head around the door and she said, "Now, now Mrs Blakeley, it's not time for you yet. This is your second baby so you should know better. We are extremely busy this morning," then she promptly disappeared. I lay there for a few minutes and pressed the buzzer yet again. Around popped her head and before she could say anything, I boldly declared that my baby's head was pushing through, so she took a look and immediately got me up on my feet, slapped an extremely large sanitary towel between my legs and almost frog marched me into the next room, which was in fact the labour room. "You can't have it here," she had declared, and it seemed that in no time at all, baby 'Garry Peter' was in my arms. I kissed and blessed him for being so gentle with me. His brother Teddy had paved the way for us both. Garry's birth had not been the drawn out painful experience that bringing his older brother into the world had been.

In the year 1956, the time of Garry's birth, one would be kept in the Nursing home or hospital for ten days. There were very limited visiting hours and no children allowed at all, and definitely only two visitors per bed. Ted visited our new baby and me every evening, but I was missing Teddy so much that Ted promised to bring him the next visit. I was to be at my window at a certain time, so that I could gaze down and drink my fill. Ted and I agreed that Teddy should not see me in case it distressed him and of course I had to miss out on my usual visit with Ted.

On the fifth day I was told I would be bathing Garry myself, and although this was my second time around, I still felt nervous. The nurse instructing me told me that in all her twenty-two years of nursing, she had never known a Mother to drop her baby. I noticed a brown marking on Garry's little chest and also on the end of his nose. "Don't worry about his nose," she said "By the time you go home we will have sorted that out, and as for the mark on his chest, it was only a birth mark," and she assured me it would not cause my baby a serious problem. I proceeded to tell her how I believed what caused it.

About half way through my pregnancy, I spilt some lighter fuel contained in a small can all over my left arm. I was sitting close to the fireplace and Ted was in the process of lighting the fire. It all happened so fast. My arm was alight, but Ted acted very quickly. He smothered my arm in his jumper that he was wearing at the time. The shock had wrenched a scream from me that must have temporarily deafened him, and as I raised my right hand to my face to stifle the scream, I remembered my Mother's warning that if I ever received any kind of shock, not to put my hands to my face. My finger just touched the tip of my nose and I had dropped my fingers to my breast. And the mark on Garry's chest fits perfectly my three fingers.

The nurse just smiled and so did my doctor when I told him at a later date. There are those who believe these old wives tales and those who don't, but nobody will ever convince me that I didn't mark my baby. But thanks to my Mum's warning and my belief in her, Garry was saved from wearing his birthmark on his face instead of his chest.

Three days before I was to be sent home, Ted arrived at visiting time and informed me that we had been offered a three-bedroom house. No. 90 Churchill Avenue, Ore Village, Hastings; it was evidence that the social services had really gone all out on our behalf.

The next three days seemed to go so slowly. I couldn't wait to get home, especially to see and hold Teddy. At sixteen months old he was still very much a baby himself and I had missed him terribly. Came the day of my departure; I thanked the nursing staff for all

97

their kindness, and said my goodbyes to everyone. One young nurse came to me and told me that the sister had claimed that I had been a model patient. The woman in the next bed to mine thought the nurse was referring to her.

"Who me?" she cried.

"No," said the nurse. "Sister said you bellowed like a bull" I went over and gave her a hug and we both ended up laughing.

The taxi arrived, and I left with baby Garry, all wrapped up in his new white shawl that my Mum had bought for him because it was the month of November and so, very cold. I was bundled into the taxi along with my small suitcase and in less than fifteen minutes arrived at home. I knocked on the door and was let in by Richard and Geoffrey with smiles all round; they claimed they were very pleased to have me home because their brother Ted's cooking was lousy. How typical of young boys to be mainly concerned with their stomachs.

Ted was holding Teddy when I arrived, so he stood him down, thereby allowing Teddy to run to me. Ted walked forward and took the baby. I held out my arms, but Teddy just stared at me and I froze. He didn't recognize me; I felt devastated. Then all of a sudden he gave a squeal of delight and with the most wonderful smile lighting up his face, he threw himself into my arms.

The next two weeks put a strain on everyone, but the excitement of moving into a house was very evident, and motivated everyone to put much effort into the preparations. With Helen's funeral behind us, and the grieving of their loss lessening as each day passed, we found ourselves arriving at No. 90 Churchill Avenue in no time. Ted inserted the key into the lock of our very own front door and we all piled in: Ted, myself, Teddy, Garry, Margaret, Richard and Geoffrey. The front bedroom would be for Ted, myself, Teddy and Garry; the two cots would just about fit in. The two boys would have the large back bedroom and Margaret the small remaining bedroom. Everyone was wandering around the house taking it all in, but Ted was to find me sitting in the bathroom. I was hit by the realisation that, for the very first time in my life, I was to enjoy the luxury of such a room. Gone forever was the old tin bath, and the toil of filling and emptying the damn thing. I was in the back bedroom that Richard and Geoffrey would be sleeping in, making up the two single beds, when I noticed the view from their window; it was quite stunning. Wide-open fields, sectioned off by hedgerows, with large beautiful trees dotted here and there. Ted came into the room at that moment. I pointed out to him what looked like a farmhouse over to our right, then I pointed to our left and asked Ted what kind of building it was that was just situated near the church.

"That darling," he said "is the crematorium."
He told me to look at the gravestones, and pointed out to me the exact area where his Mum had been buried. I felt that was indeed a very strange coincidence.

As I got to know my immediate neighbours either side of me better, I asked if I could look from their back windows, as I needed to know if I could see Helen's grave from their houses.

Needless to say, I could not. On one side a cluster of small trees blocked my view and on the other side quite high hedgerows. This gave me a lot of food for thought. "Bless you Helen," I murmured to myself.

We had no savings at all, so it was weeks before we could buy curtains for all the windows. Lace curtains, being the cheapest, were bought and put up first; at least that would give us privacy. The heavy curtains were to take us months to find the money for.

It was now the end of November 1956 and Christmas was just three weeks away. Money was now very tight. Ted's wage at this time was in the region of about seven pounds per week, and to give you a comparison, the rent was one pound, seventeen shillings, and sixpence (£1.17s.6d) per week. It seems a pittance but we managed to feed and clothe the four of us, with even the occasional trip to the pictures. We could never afford a treat like having a meal out, but just walking along the sea front, especially on a warm summer's evening sharing a bag of freshly fried chips gave me immense pleasure, and I still enjoy this treat up to the present day.

Margaret was working and readily paid for her keep, and she always did her own washing and ironing and at weekends would help me about the house. The social services paid for Richard and Geoffrey but it was barely enough; young growing boys can get through enormous amounts of food. I'd cook dishes like Toad in the Hole, i.e. sausages in batter pudding, and my meatless wonder, which became a family joke: it comprised of onions and various vegetables but was in fact very tasty. I would make a pie that held onions, potatoes and half a dozen rashers of bacon, sometimes only streaky cut up into small pieces, which again was very tasty. Bread Pudd was a favourite, but it wasn't often that there was any bread left over.

I was a little depressed at the prospect of a mean Christmas, but come Christmas day things were looking quite good. We all enjoyed a lovely lunch and exchanged little presents. Ted had even managed to bring home a Christmas tree, and a box of Christmas tree decorations. I tied three toffees together with cotton and placed several of these bunches around the tree. This was something my Mum had done when I and my brothers and sisters were to help decorate the tree. After tea in the evening, Mum would blindfold us one by one, turn us around and guide us carefully towards the tree to find a bunch of toffees, and of course she always made sure that we all succeeded. I decided to decorate the room with home made paper chains; you could buy packets of coloured and gummed strips, that were perfect to build a chain long enough to span the width of the room. They were colourful and inexpensive. However, like all Christmas's, it was soon over. Ted promised me it would be a bigger celebration next year, and he kept his promise. My own thoughts on the matter were that we had all received the best present ever, in the shape of the house that we were all coming to refer to as home, and I would often find myself in the boys back bedroom looking out of the window across to where Helen was buried and sometimes drop a tear. She had once said to me that she wouldn't want the boys to ever have to go back into care. Well, it seems she had done her bit; we were nicely secure in our new home altogether as one family thanks to her. Ted and I both were happy to play our part; it wasn't going to be easy. A lot of hard work on the part of us both would be required. With family life there's bound to be problems and we were to have our share.

Geoffrey, who was the younger of the two boys, had a cheeky personality and at times he was full of charm, but Ted and I soon became aware that all was not well with him. He was caught stealing from my purse, and even from the moneyboxes of Teddy and Garry. On another occasion, he stole Ted's gloves. They were essential to him, as his hands in the cold weather would suffer when riding his bike to and from work. I was to sit and talk to Geoffrey hoping it would open him up to me, but I had little success. No amount of affection or pleading seemed to work. At the time I was convinced it was all down to the tragic loss of his Mother. In the five years he was with us, I found the time and patience to help him. But in the end we all had no choice but to hide anything that was of value. Unfortunately this kind of behaviour carried on into his adult life. I'm happy to say he never took up crime, but we all learnt that we couldn't trust him and all agreed that Geoffrey had a real defect in his character. His sister, Margaret, would claim that her Mum had spoilt him; he was after all the baby of the family. Margaret and Richard proved themselves to be solid characters and didn't cause us any serious problems, and all three of them eventually found their individual paths to take in life. Margaret was in fact to court and marry my youngest brother Robert, making her my sister in law, twice over. But sadly this was not to last very long. It proved to be a very turbulent union; a personality clash that defied all efforts. Eventually they divorced, and both of them were to eventually meet and marry again. I'm pleased to say both of them found happiness and success in these new found relationships. During the five years that Margaret, Richard and Geoffrey were with us, you can't imagine how much cooking, washing, ironing and cleaning I coped with. I was beginning to feel more and more like my Mum. Ted was pulling his weight; he very often would have two jobs on the go and was totally unselfish by nature. The family needs were always uppermost in his mind. I firmly believe that the trust that existed between us in our relationship was that secret ingredient that makes the difference.

He knew he was possessive of me, but always claimed he trusted me completely. He would discourage any form of entertaining at home, so a social life, you could say was practically non-existent. Life in those early years for both of us was pretty all consuming. There was always too much to do to dwell on it. We loved each other, and what time there was going spare we would share with each other. He would often leave little love notes in cupboards and drawers for me to find. Because of Ted's shift work, there were times when I felt we were like passing ships in the night.

CHAPTER FOURTEEN

Galloping Cows

As Margaret was now the age of twenty, there would be the odd occasion she would offer to look out for her two younger brothers whilst Ted, I and our two babies would go off for a little break; sometimes even for the day. It was on one of these occasions that we set out to visit the family, who were currently working in the Cherry Orchard gathering the season's fruit. We caught the bus to Tenterden, and then set out down the country road with the babes in their pushchair until we came to the farm. I told Ted we could cut across a couple of fields to save us time and energy as long as we secured the gates behind us. I must say he was very hesitant but I didn't think too much about it, and finally convinced him that it made sense. On entering the second field we began by walking up a steep slope, and to the right of us was a deep dip in the landscape so we were unable to see the dozen or so cows that were contentedly chewing away at the grass. I realised later that the cows were more aware of us than we were of them. Maybe it was near milking time, or maybe cows are naturally drawn to humans (seeing as most of them are after all domesticated animals) but whatever the reason was, these cows were making a beeline for us, and at quite a trot. Although this did not perturb me in any way, Ted began to increase his pace and pushing a pram up hill in a grassy field was not easy. Teddy was showing signs of stress so I picked him up and struggled to keep up with Ted. Needless to say we out ran the cows and secured the gate. I turned to Ted and asked him what was that all about. He dismissed the question altogether and continued to make his way towards the Cherry Orchard. I caught up with him and accused him of being afraid of cows.

"Absolutely not," he proclaimed.

By this time we were surrounded by family members who were extremely pleased to see us. However, my suspicions were confirmed at a later date, whilst on a fishing trip with the boys. Some cows made their appearance quite suddenly. Believe me, you have never seen fishing rods and picnic goodies gathered up so fast, and everything including us bundled into the car and headed out for home. I sat in the car smiling to myself. Ted never said a word, and I resisted the temptation to say to him, "I told you so". But he knew his secret was out; that the sight of cows galloping towards him was more than he cared to experience.

It was on one of these weekend visits to the Orchard that my sister Mary and her husband Eric arrived in their little Morris Minor. They had arrived Friday evening, only for Dad to tell her he had to visit home and check on the yard. He said it would be great if he could leave early Saturday morning. This would enable him to arrive back early evening on that same day. Mary, as usual always eager to be of help in any way, told Dad that she and Eric would take Mum to the shops in Tenterden leaving him free to go home to check on the yard and would look forward to having him back for the evening's festivities. These would consist of either a lively evening spent in the local pub or a singsong around the campfire.

As Friday evening was the end of everyone's week of work, there was quite a lot to get done and as usual everyone finally went off to bed totally exhausted. The fact that Mary had forgotten to mention to Eric about the Saturday morning shopping trip wasn't all that important. I mean, after all, he wasn't going anywhere. Mary had slept along side Mum and Eric in with the boys. Dad had already left for home, so all that was needed was a good strip wash and a set of clean clothes, then off to Tenterden for their shopping trip. Mary threw open the hut door and there they stood, her and Mother all done up in their Sunday best, only to find that Eric had decided to remove a rear tyre and was in the process of cleaning the wheel – and he was himself in rather a greasy state. Mary's face was a picture: utter amazement and disbelief. But Eric, bless him, put the tyre back on, cleaned himself up and in less than an hour was ready and at their bidding. Not a cross word passed between them apart from Mary's exclamation - "Oh Marty!" Just one of those situations where silence is golden.

CHAPTER FIFTEEN

Brothers

1959, and my second child Garry is three years old and he is diagnosed with having croup. You feel that nobody can understand the sheer terror that grips you when the fear for your baby's life - it fills every fibre of your being. It is torment, to watch the child you love more than your own self, struggle for breath. You know that you have done everything you can, and all that's left is to sit a silent vigil. You watch and wait for the crisis to pass and only then will you allow someone to take over whilst you sleep the sweet sleep of exhaustion.

The following year, Teddy and Garry both went down with measles. Teddy was recovering when Garry started sprouting spots, so it was at least five weeks in all that I was playing at Florence Nightingale, running up and down the stairs all day long. Whilst they both had a temperature, they were not ill enough to frighten me.

Garry complained that Teddy wouldn't hold his hand, so I took out a pair of their white ankle socks and placed one on each of their hands. Teddy was mumbling something about having enough spots of his own, without catching Garry's, but he was happy to hold Garry's hand once the socks were in place. As by this time Richard and Geoffrey had both left home, Teddy and Garry now occupied the back bedroom, and I would go up to check on them making sure they had settled down and gone off to sleep. I would find that they had pushed the beds together, and had indeed gone off to sleep holding hands. I firmly believe that it was Garry who had instigated this turn of events. This continued for a number of years. It was in these early years that a strong brotherly bond was built between them. It still exists to this very day, although in their mid teens they both began to show how different they were from each other, by selecting completely different roles in life.

Teddy was over the measles and up and about before his brother, and I made the mistake of giving Garry a stick to enable him to bang on the floor if he needed me. He wasn't very happy being left up there on his own. By the end of the second day, I called up the stairs and told him,

"If you bang that stick one more time, I'll be up and thrash you with a feather!"

"Feathers won't hurt me!" he answered.

"You haven't seen the size of my feather!"

But my heart softened and I made a little bed with chairs in the dining room, so he could see me in the kitchen preparing the evening meal.

Then of course came 'Chicken Pox'. I was constantly pleading with them not to scratch. Then came 'Mumps', and everyone told me that I should be pleased that they had caught Mumps young because it would be far worse for them in adult life. Apparently it is a very painful experience for a man.

Teddy and Garry, although having different personalities developing, got on very well. There was just sixteen months difference between their ages and I believe this was an asset.

Teddy was now five years old and quite ready to go off to school in his brand new uniform. A week went by and everyone said how lucky I was that he'd taken to it so well. So the following Monday, off we set again, Teddy helping me to push Garry along in his pushchair. On arriving at the school main entrance, Garry and I waved to Teddy until he slowly disappeared into the building. If anyone was unhappy, it was Garry. I decided I would spend more time playing with him. I had always sat with them both and watched 'Children's Hour'. There was 'Andy Pandy', not forgetting 'The Flowerpot Men' and their garden friend 'Weed'. But a favourite was story time and was called 'Watch with Mother'. So on arriving back home I set about cheering Garry up before tackling my household chores; he soon rallied round. It was about one thirty in the afternoon - I had the back door open and I heard the patter of little shoes approaching. I watched and waited to see who would pop their head around. In the open door was none other than Teddy. I looked behind him expecting a teacher to have brought him home, but to my horror I realised he had crossed two very busy roads on his own. I asked him what he was doing coming home. He told me how he thought school was very nice but he had had enough now and wanted to stay at home.

I sat him down and tried to explain what going to school was all about - not easy to understand when you're only five. I took him back to school, but it seemed hardly worth it as the day was nearly over. His teacher said I had done the right thing. I felt the need to express my disapproval of the fact that it was even possible for a five year old to just walk off. I believe that security was consequently tightened up, but the school could not recall any child other than Teddy ever doing such a thing. The next day I dropped Teddy into school in a very distressed state. The teacher promised me that as soon as I was gone he would settle down. As I left the building, I could hear him crying and calling out for me. I arrived home and spent the day feeling miserable and guilty. At last it was time to collect him and bring him home. I waited at the school entrance for him to appear. Out he came, skipping and smiling, full of chatter about what he had been doing all day - proving the teacher right. To think I had spent such a miserable day unnecessarily.

I decided I would have to find the time somehow to take Garry to playschool and thereby prepare him for his primary schooling. This I did, and Garry seemed to have no problems at all, but he did have Teddy at play and lunch times - which again I felt that Teddy, for the second time, had paved the way for Garry. The first time being Garry's easier birthing compared with his older brother's painful arrival.

As time went by they grew very close and would often be seen holding hands and would play together happily. I regularly invited playmates into the garden rather than let them play out on the street. As they grew older it became obvious to me that I would have to relent and allow them to venture outside the gate to play; then came the squabbles. Teddy was very protective of Garry, to a point of Garry making a tearful and even angry protest: he wanted to be able

107

to fight his own battles, and not have Teddy always grabbing him, taking him down to the ground and sitting on him. I explained to Teddy how frustrating this could be for his younger brother, and in future to allow Garry to fight his own battles. However, if he ever saw two boys giving his brother a bad time he could be supportive by pinning one on the ground to even things up, so long as it wasn't on Garry! My little chat with Teddy paid off.

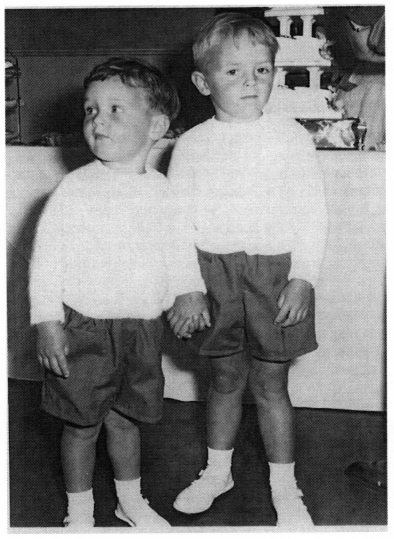

Garry and Teddy

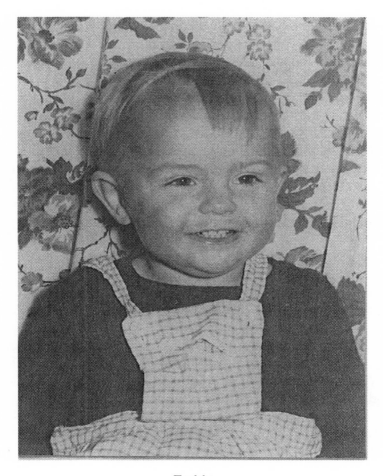

Teddy

These street squabbles were rare and generally the children all played very well together and many friendships were formed that lasted for years, and I learnt that there was safety in numbers, and no matter how much you would like to wrap your children up in cotton wool, you have to slowly, bit by bit allow them to spread out and grow. It's very important to allow them to become street wise, and you just hope that the love, discipline and trust that you've instilled in them brings them through to adult life.

At the age of seven, Garry was to come home from school one day stating that there were four violins, and any child who would like to learn to play was to get permission from their parents. He was very adamant that he should be allowed to take a note saying that Ted and I approved and would make regular payments until the violin was paid for in full. Money was always scarce, but I promised Garry I would speak to his Dad that very evening and let him know in the morning whether or not it would be possible. When putting the boys to bed, Garry was again to plead with me, "Please Mum, I really want to play the violin". I kissed him on the forehead and promised to plead on his behalf. The boys often had to accept a 'No', but as I reminded Ted later that evening, we both agreed that saying no sometimes helped to build character. But on this occasion, I knew it had to be a yes. Garry had never asked for anything and somehow my instincts told me this was really important to him - he really wanted one of those violins. I'm happy to say that Ted was in full agreement with me. After all, we could always sell the instrument if Garry decided at a later date that he'd had enough.

Garry proved to be really dedicated and never had to be encouraged ever to study his music or practice on the violin. He had to tolerate a certain amount of teasing. One day coming home from school, a couple of his fellow school boys quipped, "Still on the fiddle then Garry," to which he replied "yes, and I can still fight". The boys walked away laughing. Garry proved time and time again he was not going to be deterred from learning to play his violin.

The Violin must be the world's most difficult instrument to learn and it demands a lot of dedication; it's not too kind on the eardrums either, but I remember the day when Garry's playing stopped me mid way coming down the stairs. He was actually playing music. I went dashing into Ted crying, "He's got it. Our boy has got it". Ted just smiled at me and said, "Of course he has. Don't tell me you ever had any doubts". And I don't believe I did.

Teddy at this time was nine years old and developing quite a strong will and character, and with good parenting these two factors could prove to serve him well. He also had an abundance of charm and its true to say that he did give his Dad and myself a need to give him much attention. Where his brother Garry had selected a Violin as his choice of musical instrument, Teddy decided he would like to play the Guitar. In time Ted was able to purchase a second-hand one for him; the make was a Gibson, red in colour and in excellent condition. Teddy was ecstatic when we handed it over to him along with 'Book 1 for Learners'. We were to listen for results but would find him on his bed strumming away to some of his favourite music, and no amount of encouragement was to steer him towards actually learning to play it by the book. Eventually the phase passed and he moved on to something else. This is the pattern that Teddy was to apply with most things as he was growing up; he wanted to try many things, and did.

Garry aged thirteen years

Garry was to plod along with his Violin very happily and with a determination that paid off. It was never a chore for him; he enjoyed the challenge and the results. Quite often he would come to me and state that he was going to be joining in on a game of football or just going to the playing fields with his friends. I always encouraged him to take time out. I always felt that it was a good idea for him not to become too obsessed with his music. Its always amazed me that Garry had found his notch, so to speak, at such a very young age; he was so different to his brother Teddy. Garry was somewhat laid back about everything, but very positive about what he wanted, and its true to say he hardly ever caused his father or myself any anxieties, which is just as well. If we had had two high-spirited boys instead of just one, it could have proved to be very draining.

Time eased forward at a steady pace, and eventually at the age of eleven Teddy was to move on to secondary school. He was a very well adjusted boy, so I was surprised when he came home from school one day and proceeded to tell me of a classmate who had run away from home because he had found out by accident that he was adopted, and that even the police had been up to the school making enquiries. I explained to Teddy that it must have been a terrible shock for the boy to find out that way.

"If I had been adopted what would you have done Mum?" he asked. I thought for a few moments before I decided I would tell a child at the age of three years old, saying that I would in fact have looked amongst hundreds of children until I had found a special one that was right - just for me. Teddy thought about this and then asked if he was adopted.

"No darling," I said, "you were not".

"Will you show me my birth certificate Mum?" I went upstairs to dig out the shoebox that I kept all my special documents in and showed him his birth certificate. I smiled at him and asked if there was anything else he would like to see while we were with the shoebox.

"May I see your marriage certificate Mum?"

"Yes, you may," and I stood there while he counted off the months on his fingers. I very quickly realized he was counting the months between the date of my marriage and his birth. I didn't want him worrying, but I did say to him that I very much hoped that as he grew older he would learn to trust my word and not find it necessary to question it. He kissed me and said sorry, telling me he already trusted me. I believe his concern for his classmate followed by curiosity got the better of him. There was no repeat of distrust concerning 'my word' ever again.

Ted often teased the boys playfully and they would run to me and ask if their Dad was teasing or telling the truth. I decided that one teaser in the family was enough, and always set the dispute to rights which ended up with Ted and the boys having a tumble. But there was one occasion when I allowed Ted to talk me into playing a joke on the boys. They were both very fond of a Weetabix breakfast, especially Garry. There was a time when I thought he would have eaten it, not only for breakfast, but for lunch and dinner as well. Ted told them that the Weetabix lorry had broken down and the factory was closing down so there would never be anymore Weetabix. Garry came running to me for confirmation and when I agreed with his Dad, he became very upset, and I immediately put his mind at rest and promised him faithfully I would never again join in on his Dads games; even Ted realized we had both made a mistake.

One joker in the family was always going to be fine, but two parents were definitely proved to be a no.

When the time came for Garry to follow his older brother and move on to Secondary Schooling, Ted and I sat and discussed that it would be more beneficial for him to be placed at a school where his musical talents would be best encouraged. At this moment in time, The Grove School was well known for the work they were doing with music. Though we were concerned about sending him to a different school, we could well imagine Garry becoming part of the Orchestra that The Grove was very proud of. As the years passed, I do believe he had to take quite an amount of teasing, but he survived, and it probably helped to build the strong character that he has today. I learnt very young that very little if anything could be done to change a personality, but a child's character could be built as long as they had a loving and supporting family around them. They would be able to overcome the knocks in life.

So now that Teddy and Garry were happily settled in their schools, my Mum was to suggest to me that it was high time that Ted and myself should think about taking a short holiday on our own, and that she would have the boys. We had never left the children before and I was quite unable to contemplate doing so now. Ted pointed out to me that I couldn't leave them with just anybody, but surely the boys would come to no harm with Mum. So it was agreed that we took a week's holiday touring Wales, relying on bed and breakfast wherever we found ourselves at the end of each day. Ted promised to include the part of Wales where I had been evacuated to during World War II. Ted and I were both aware that our marriage was beginning to show signs of strain, and that a week together on our own would be very good for us.

Money being scarce, holidays had always been last on the agenda, but we took a couple of holidays with the children in Ireland and stayed with an auntie of Ted's. It is a beautiful country but I somehow found it quite, 'damp'. Irish bread was something to die for; I remember thinking it was more like a cake. I found the people very friendly and very family orientated. At the end of the road where we were staying there was a church on one side and a public house on the other, and I'd always been led to understand that the Irish were very religious people. I found it odd to see the men on a Sunday coming out of church and popping across the road to disappear into the pub. The 'Mountains of Mourn' I never did see because each trip was to find the mountains covered in mist. The one and only holiday we had when we would stay at a Guesthouse, again with the boys, was when we booked a week down the West Country, but this proved to be a stressful time for Ted. He constantly worried that the children might be too noisy. It became very noticeable to staff, especially at meal times, that Ted was not enjoying himself. The owner was to approach him on about the third day, requesting him to relax and ensuring him the children were behaving very well. Her talking to him proved to be helpful, but I am certain that Ted was glad to be going home. On the last day we went down to the Quay to give the boys one last look at all the beautiful boats and to enjoy one last local ice-cream. Ted led us all to the shops and I stopped to look in a Jewellers window and pointed out a lovely silver ring with quite a large amethyst stone. I just sighed and we walked on. I knew that money should not be spent on such things. I suggested to Ted that he amuse the boys while I packed and made ready for our departure.

On their return Ted took me to one side and gave me a little square box. Upon lifting the lid, I saw the ring that I had so admired in the Jewellers shop window. He had slipped back to the shop and bought it for me. He believed that apart from my wedding and engagement ring he had never bought me any jewellery, so therefore I was not to moan at him. Birthdays and Christmases were to bring to me other pieces of jewellery from him that I still have and treasure to this very day.

CHAPTER SIXTEEN

Wales Revisited

Having hugged and extracted promises from the boys to be good for their Nan, Ted and I set off on our wandering holiday in the direction of South Wales and the hope that the week would serve to put some new life into our marriage.

Ted had worked out a route taken from a rather dated map of South Wales, so we should not have been surprised to find many landmarks changed. I was to experience many disappointments.

I've heard it said many times that one shouldn't go back to visit one's memories, as one runs the risk of distorting those memories. In those first three days I shed many tears. Ted was able to find the Scouts Hall that had been home to Mum and five of us kids. It was deserted and in a dilapidated state. Gone was the front veranda that had always had a lovely show of wild roses. The windows were either cracked or broken. When Ted hoisted me up to peer inside, I felt a stab of pain in my chest and the tears just flowed. Worse was to come. As I have mentioned before, this hall had been built smack in the middle of Lord and lady Gilbertson's land. Gone were the garden fetes, thoroughbred horses, the well-kept grass fields, the boating lake and boathouse, and the field of cultured and cared for Christmas Trees. The pure beauty of the place that I remembered was all gone. The big house was still there, but as if my misery was to be made complete, it had been renovated into several flats. It was at this point that Ted could take no more of my distress. "Enough is enough," he declared and proceeded to march me away, back out of the rusty large gate that had once been so majestic in appearance and had played its part in making us feel safe and secure. Upon reaching the car, I asked Ted if he would join me in one last thing before whisking me away. It was the walk I had to take many times in the school lunch hour to collect sandwiches for us all, and would arrive back at the school with barely enough time for us to eat them. I had boasted many times, in my adult life of this great fete of endurance, and told of it with much pride. So imagine my amazement when the walk from the Hall to the school only took twelve minutes, but at least there were no tears shed.

Nothing on the route had changed at all; even the little spinney with the wooden steps that led up to the school entrance was still there. That twelve-minute walk was to serve me as a soothing balm and brought a smile back to my face and a sigh of relief from Ted. On the walk back to the Car I thanked him for his understanding and tolerance, and gave a promise to stop at the first suitable place to have some lunch. I suddenly remembered that he had complained of hunger pangs an hour previously.

After a satisfying meal we set off. I was determined to track down a young girl who had been our babysitter on occasions when Mum went shopping to our nearest town Ystradgynlias. We had all been very fond of her, and the idea of meeting her again filled me with a warm glow.

She had in fact moved from the premises where I had expected to find her, but a local shop owner was very happy to help when he realised I was an evacuee revisiting, and so he furnished me with her new address. With bated breath I got out of the car and walked up the path, and knocked upon the front door. I don't quite know what I expected, but it wasn't what I actually got. The door opened, and although the girl had become a woman, there was something there that made her instantly recognisable to me. I told her who I was, but there was no real reaction at all.

"O' hello," she said. She was completely cold. I felt at the time that she seemed quite indifferent. It was as if she had punched me in the belly. It would have helped if she had at least invited us in and offered a cup of tea, and perhaps a little chat about old times. It was obvious that she had not carried with her any special memories at all. I felt hurt to say the least and after a couple of minutes on the doorstep, I felt obliged to leave. I wished her well and returned to the car. Ted drove off in silence as if he was allowing me time to lick my wounds. Yes, I felt hurt. Whilst I had nurtured fond memories of her, I realised that us kids had just been a means of earning a bit of pocket money to her. Nothing wrong in that in itself, but I had been totally unprepared for it.

Well, tomorrow is another day I thought, and after a tasty meal and a good nights sleep, we set out once again. I remember it being a lovely sunny day and the adventure into my childhood past was still up and running, and as I was now on ground that was familiar to me, I gave Ted directions that would hopefully find a lovely little wishing well that us kids would occasionally throw the old penny in and make wonderful wishes. And, sure enough, there it was, still where I knew it would be. Ted pulled the car over and before he had completely stopped, I was placing my feet on the pavement and then rushing over to the well. I knew I was behaving like some over excited child, but I couldn't help myself. I was so excited to find it. Ted joined me and he had a big grin on his face. He obviously found my behaviour very amusing. Having calmed down, I looked around for the landmarks I knew should be there. I found myself literally spinning around in the middle of the road. I became confused; something was wrong. Then very slowly I began to realise that certain drastic changes had taken place. Where there had once stood a row of whitewashed cottages there was now overgrown wasteland. The field and wooded area that had been blessed with many very large beautiful trees and where us kids had spent many happy days playing and running free was also gone. In its place had been laid a very impressive major road that stretched as far as the eye could see. After my unhappy experiences of the previous day, I should have been more prepared to find changes, but my heart was sinking. Then suddenly, I realized that the stream that had run parallel to the field should still be there. After all, the power of flowing water would prove to be too much of a costly project to re-route. I ran across the road with Ted hot on my heels. At this stage, he had no idea what was going through my mind. I leaned over the railings and there it was. At least there was no change there. Fast flowing water bubbling and trickling over cobble stones, clear clean water that was no more than a few inches deep; therefore as safe as any place could be for children to play. We even fished, but not with rod and line; we fished using our bare hands. Small fat little fish, that were many in number, and they would mostly hide under stones. With practice, you could become very successful at it. While standing straddle legged and hands cupped under the water, you would give a nod to your fishing partner, which was an indication for them to lift a large cobble stone allowing a fish to dart out. If you were lucky, it would dart straight into your cupped hands.

We always set them free because we had no desire to hurt them, only to experience the challenge of the hunt.

I remember the boys tying a length of rope to the branch of a tree, then one at a time we would grab the rope, take several steps back and once our feet left the ground, the rope would take us flying through the air and out over the water. Even after all those years, I could feel the exhilaration that I had experienced at that time.

The life and love that I had shared with my blood siblings in such unsettling times often leaves me to wonder what it would have been like to have been born an only child. Its true to say that I really have no idea; I only know that such thoughts would leave me feeling somewhat melancholy but, there is also a sense of gratitude that we were always able to stay together during those five years of 'War Torn England', when thousands of families had been ripped apart for practically the entire duration of that war. It's true to say we saw very little of Dad, but Mum would tell us that it was never Dad's fault, and it became something that we all learnt very quickly to accept.

There was still one other person I desperately wanted to find, but Ted and I decided it should wait until tomorrow, and we spent the rest of that day just sightseeing. Wales is a beautiful country and both of us delighted in just driving around and stopping at various locations to take in and enjoy some really beautiful countryside.

As the sun rose on the third day of our travels, we set out to track down a female named Betty Phue. She had been the adopted daughter of a couple who owned and ran the farm that had been situated right next to the Gilbertson's estate. They also had an older legitimate daughter that I never really got to know a lot about. Betty had been a good friend and playmate, and I would often be invited over to the farm to play. I remember one occasion when together we had rigged up a sort of stage in a barn with the idea of putting on a show that would project our talents. Betty and I, along with two other girls, practiced together and also built a temporary stage. The show comprised of a selection of singing and dancing. We advertised at our local school and charged one-penny entrance fee. With the after school performance time and date set, we were up and running. The sale of seats was somewhat daunting having only sold eight seats, but we were still prepared for the show to be performed. At eleven years old the most important thing to me at that time was to play the part. With our audience settled a small boy, as pre-arranged, pulled back the pair of curtains that Betty's parents had supplied for the event. Betty and I entered the stage left, and before we had barely began, the whole stage completely collapsed. Fortunately neither of us was hurt, but at such a tender age the embarrassment alone was enough to bear. So we very rightly returned said pennies, and both of us returned home with our tails between our legs. But as is usual with healthy young people, our disappointment was soon forgotten.

Having finally discovered where she was living, and given the information that she was married with one child (a young daughter) I once again found myself with much apprehension knocking on the front door of a terraced house. A woman answered to my knocking; she was plump and had a round happy smiling face.

I saw nothing there that was to remind me of my young friend and playmate. But when I told her who I was and who I was looking for, she proceeded to jump up and down with so much glee, I instantly realized that I had in fact found the one I had been searching for.

She dragged me into the house and began screeching and squawking to her family and declaring that she knew one day I would re-enter her life. Our happiness and excitement spread throughout her family. Even her Dad who lived next door and had always said that an English spoken person would not be welcome over his threshold, made an exception to his rule by making me feel very welcome. Sadly Betty's Mother had long passed away. She later was to confirm to me that although she had been adopted, she was in fact the daughter of her supposed sister and of course in those days friends and neighbours scorned a pregnant unmarried woman, so her Mother and father solved the problem by officially adopting Betty. Not only did she make us a cup of tea, she insisted on cooking us something to eat, and was adamant that Ted and I sleep the night. After a couple of hours chatting, she took us upstairs and showed us into the spare bedroom. She apologized for the fact that only one half of the window had been fitted with a curtain, and proceeded to pull the wardrobe around at an angle to ensure us both suitable privacy. She told us that her husband, when he was ready, would "shit another miracle" and put up the other half of the curtain. We told her not to be concerned and assured her that the welcome we had received was overwhelming and nothing else was of any importance.

The next morning I was to discover that she was in fact a qualified District Nurse and she asked if I would like to join her on her morning round. I accepted, with a promise to Ted that we would set off once again before evening and darkness set in. As Betty and I set out on her morning visits, she told me that there was one elderly gentleman for whom it would be best if I waited in the car. She promised not to keep me waiting too long. Apparently this particular gentleman could quite possibly embarrass me. The most she would tell me was that he was a frisky old man who she had to bathe, and he constantly sexually propositioned her, and that she often had to "slap him down". When she told me he was eighty-three years old, I was somewhat surprised to say the least. Betty claimed it was all part of the job. I certainly found the morning round very interesting and could quite understand why she enjoyed her job so much. Not only was it a very rewarding job, but also it was often very amusing.

Betty would have liked me to stay longer, but I knew Ted was ready to move on. So with hugs and drawn out farewells, Ted and I left this happy little family with promises to write. I was to carry away with me a great sense of achievement and a happiness that stayed with me for a very long time.

I was very aware that the last three days had proved to be a bit of a strain on Ted; hunting down particular landmarks and seeking out particular people. At that time Ted had to do all the driving because at this point I had not as yet learnt to drive. So the rest of the week was to be more relaxed and less driving for Ted. I was determined not to make any more demands on him. After all, this was a holiday for him as well.

On the sixth day, my map reading was to prove to be the one and only time I let Ted down. He was very good about it because we were most definitely lost and the prospect of finding sleeping accommodation as night drew in was getting very slim. I informed Ted that I was feeling very tired, and asked if we couldn't just stop and sleep in the car.

"Very unwise," he declared.

But as if by magic we came upon an opening in the hedge and Ted just drove straight onto a field, and parked the car alongside the hedgerow that placed us out of sight of anyone that would be driving along the main road. Our car at this time was a seven year old Austin 1800 and the rear seats would fold down to provide a very comfortable temporary bed. With the two rugs that we had thrown in the back of the car on our departure to keep us warm, we were convinced we would spend a comfortable night. With the smell of freshly cut hay in our nostrils, and the light of a full moon, it was to prove to be a very romantic setting. And although I can't possibly swear to it, I have always been convinced that that was the night I fell pregnant with my third child, Darran. Let's call it a woman's intuition.

We arrived home to the great delight of Teddy and Garry; it was obvious that the boys had missed us both very much. We soon all settled down and life fell back into its usual pattern. I had missed the boys so much, I declared that I would never leave them for more than a day ever again, and I never did. Although I couldn't regret having revisited the place of my childhood, it is true to say that I was no longer able to hang on to my original memories; they became clouded over. My new experiences of my recent holiday were to take precedence in my thoughts.

When my monthly cycle did not appear, I made an appointment to see my doctor. Although it was too soon for him to diagnose whether I was pregnant or not, I was feeling a certain amount of panic. Good grief, I was 35 years old, and I was asking myself "can I cope with this?" My doctor said there was no need for me to worry at all. A law had just been passed in the Houses of Parliament that any woman 35 years or over would automatically be entitled to an abortion on the NHS. The mention of that word, 'abortion' sent shivers down my spine. I could never undertake to make that kind of decision.

"If that's the case," said my doctor "Why are you in such a panic?"

"Dr Ingham," I declared, "At thirty-five years old, I think I'm entitled to panic if I want to." He just smiled, and told me to go home and to come back and see him in about six weeks when at such time he would be able to confirm whether I was pregnant or not.

So it was that the following year in the month of May, my third and last son was born. I remember the first time I held him in my arms; he'd been bathed and powdered and smelt the only way that newborn babies can smell. He had two fingers in his mouth and one up his nose; not exactly the picture to carry through life with you, but it made me smile then, and still does every time I think about it. I have often wondered, if Ted and I had not taken the trip to Wales, and had not parked for the night in a farmer's field, would Darran in fact ever had been born?

I perish the thought.

CHAPTER SEVENTEEN

Mum & Dad Break-up

Mum's health over the last few years had rapidly become worse, and us three girls between us had helped her out at times when she was forced to take to her bed.

Antibiotics would soon clear up Mum's chest infection, but they always left her feeling drained and very depressed. Dad would happily see to her basic needs, but he was never very good around sickness - not the type to sit and hold her hand. He would go about his daily routine, and I daresay he did not provide much company for her at these times. These bouts of illnesses gradually became more frequent and more intolerable for her to bear. So came the day when Mother put on her coat and made her way to me.

I was in the kitchen washing up dishes when the knock on the door came. The minute I saw her face I knew she was upset and was once again unwell. I put her to bed, made her a cup of tea, and once I felt she was comfortable I phoned for the doctor. When he arrived he made his examination and wrote out the usual prescription, and as he was about to walk out of the front door, he solemnly informed me that my Mum was going to need some serious looking after. Suddenly, the penny dropped; that was why she had come to me instead of phoning in the usual way. Later I phoned Dad and assured him she was okay, and that I would pop round in the morning to pack some clean clothes.

"Tell your mum," he said, "I'll be round to see her in the morning. And don't worry about me, I can look after myself; just you look out for your Mum".

The doctor had been right; it was three weeks before Mum was well enough to go back home. But that was when Mum quietly informed me that she didn't want to go home again, ever.

"I can't cope anymore my love," she said, "Life has become all too much for me. I want to stay home here with you".

Ted was very fond of my Mum but he was concerned about how Dad would react to such news. I told Ted I was going to talk to Dad in the morning. I wasn't expecting Dad to be difficult, but felt sure it would come as a bit of a shock. It turned out that he was very understanding and agreed with me that it would be best for Mum.

"I don't want her to leave home and if she improves enough, the door will always be open for her" he declared.

Dad came twice a week to visit with us, and he would chat away to Mum while I busied myself about the house to give them space. He never ever said, but I was certain that he missed her. Mum always looked forward to his visits, but she never ever gave any indication that she would like to move back home.

It was very obvious to me that they still cared very much for one another, but it was also very obvious to me that Mum had reached a point in her life where her health was draining her bodily energies, and that her doctor had been right on the button when he had told me she was going to need considerable care. This was no problem for me; I loved Mum very much, and it was fortunate that Ted was ready to give me his full support.

I should mention at this point that both my sisters and their partners would have been happy to do the same. The fact that Mum had come to me proved to be rather painful for my sister Mary. She asked why Mum had come to me, and not to her. It was her opinion that she had always been Mum's girl and I had been Dads. Mum loved us all with a fierce passion, and so it was, as time went by, that I came to the conclusion that because I was very much like my father in many ways, being with me in some strange way kept her closer to the man she had left, but still loved.

CHAPTER EIGHTEEN

Pregnancy at Thirty-Five

The fact that Mum was now living with us at a time when I was about two months into my pregnancy, served as a calming influence on both Ted and myself, and we found ourselves really looking forward to this new addition to our family. Teddy at this time was aged about thirteen and my Garry, eleven years and six months. They both had taken the news with nothing more than an element of surprise, and didn't seem at all put out. Several months previously Ted, in answer to my pleas, stuck 'L' plates on the front and back of our Austin 1800, allowing me to take the steering wheel. He endeavoured to teach me to drive. It's true to say his patience was really put to the test. I remember the occasion when having driven to Rye. We were on the return trip when Ted's patience with me was completely lost. He jumped out of the car, snatched the "L" plates off and threw them over the hedge.

"I'll drive the rest of the way home," he declared, and in no uncertain terms instructed me to move over. Now it was my turn to jump out of the car, and with an indignant air and my chin pushed forward, I proceeded to walk. And I was determined to walk the entire four miles home.

"Don't be foolish," Ted said and suggested I get back into the car.
After several attempts he gave up and drove off. About half an hour had gone by and to my horror it began to rain. At this point Ted decided to double back, and try once again to coax me back into the car. If he had felt inclined to apologise for his shouting at me, I'm sure I would have, but he was inclined to grin at me which made me feel stupid, so I completely ignored him and was even more determined to walk all the way home.

The rain did not ease up and by the time I arrived home I was soaking wet. I let myself into the house by means of the back door, which Ted had left unlocked. He knew I was not carrying my key with me. He was sitting in a chair that was facing the door, so it was that as I stepped into the room our eyes clashed. There I stood dripping wet from the top of my head to my water logged shoes. After a few seconds he just burst out laughing and then walked towards me and put his arms around me. He muttered something about me being a right stubborn little cow, but it seemed to me there was a spark of admiration in his eyes as well. I got my apology, but nevertheless I decided I would forget the idea of learning to drive - at least until we could afford for me to have lessons.

So it was agreed upon that I should book up eight lessons and hopefully pass the final test before my pregnancy reached the advance stages. I studied the Highway Code book every day without fail. Ted had been the family taxi driver for so long, that I do believe he was looking forward to the day when I would be able to share the load.

Before I was five months pregnant I took my test and passed. I drove home and pulled up to a stop outside the house. Ted was working in the front garden. I called out to him that I was now a qualified driver, looking for at least some form of congratulations.

Instead, he carried on digging, with the suggestion I go pick up the groceries, but I could tell by the smile on his face that he was really pleased for me.

My brother John was in the area and so he decided to pop in for a cup of tea and a chat. He found me out the back chopping a log of wood into small sticks.

"The boiler fire is almost out" I told him, "And I'm hoping to save it".
Ted arrived from work at this point and took the small axe off me.

"You shouldn't be doing jobs like this in your condition," he said.
My brother offered to take the axe and bring it back the next day, sharpened. "For god sake, don't do that," said Ted. "My Bett is so cack-handed, she's bound to chop her arm off."
Needless to say, John decided not to take the axe.

I came to the conclusion that I could almost get away with murder while pregnant, but I sincerely hope I didn't consciously take advantage. But one thing I remember is that Ted was not going to let me get away with driving the car at the end of my pregnancy.

"Your stomach is pressing up against the steering wheel," he declared "And you are not to drive the car".

Mum quietly agreed with him, so between them and my own common sense I gave in. I knew they were both right.

In less than a fortnight Darran made his presence known. The sister who had been present at the birth declared, "This child of yours is going to be very strong, he has a grip of steel". And time itself was to prove her right.

Pregnancy at thirty-five proved to be a total success. Mother and baby doing well, I was sent home after only five days. In those five days my Mother had proved to be a great help to Ted - keeping the home ticking over in my absence.

On my arrival home, I barely had the chance to introduce Mother to her latest grandchild when I realised that the anticipation and excitement of my arrival home was a little too much for her. I passed the baby over to Ted and gently led Mum upstairs to bed to rest a while. On my arrival back downstairs, Ted seemed amazed to say the least and proclaimed that Mum had been quite well when he had left home that morning. Bronchitis can be like that - and as time went by I found I was able to detect the threat of its arrival even before Mother.

All aspects of Mum's life could trigger off a complaint: stress, excitement, shock and even joy. I had to watch her closely. My sisters were always there helping, and my brothers claimed they were only a phone call away. We were all prepared to give back something of the love and care that Mum had always given to us. Dad, home and her children, including grandchildren, was all that she lived for. When writing about her I always feel such deep felt emotions, and almost humble to have been part of a woman that had such a capacity to love and to give so unselfishly of herself.

CHAPTER NINETEEN

My Son Teddy

Teddy, now approaching the age of fourteen, was developing a great capacity and zest for life. Whilst he still had that mischievous twinkle in his eye, he was beginning to express himself with a determination and will that was to keep his Dad and myself forever on our toes.

He had an abundance of mental and physical energy, but did not seem to be directing it in any particular direction. His school reports were always a good average, but stated he was capable of so much more.

The day came for him to leave school and at sixteen he still had no idea what he wanted to do. Ted and I became very concerned. But as always the sun came out for Teddy whenever a cloud hung over his head. A chat over the garden hedge with our friendly neighbour brought about the offer of an apprenticeship as a toolmaker, with one day a week attending a local college. Whilst Teddy found the work interesting enough, a factory type environment didn't seem to suit him terribly well. He would come home sometimes looking pale and sickly. I suggested he spent his break times outside in the fresh air; this proved to help a little. I pleaded with him to stick it out and complete his apprenticeship, with a promise that once he had passed his City & Guilds exam, he would receive no opposition from Ted or myself regarding what his next move would be.

"Okay Mum" he said, "I know I can make it."

Two years later, he certainly did. He came home one day and proudly dropped said papers into my lap.

"Well now darling, are you going to stick with it?" I asked.

"No Mum," he replied, "I've already given in my notice at work. Everyone there said they were very sorry to see me go, and all wished me well, and hoped I would do well in the future."

"Talking of your future my son, have you anything in mind that you would like to do?"

"Yes" he said, "I've already got a job working outside in the open air. I've been told I can start as soon as I have served out my notice"

I was disappointed, but I graciously gave him my blessing. At eighteen, he was very much a young man and the reigns were off.

For almost a year he had been courting a petite and pretty Irish girl. As she was only fifteen, I was somewhat concerned and ventured to speak to Teddy and to warn him of the consequences should Teresa fall pregnant.

"Don't worry Mum," he said, "Everything is well under control."
Famous last words if I ever heard them.

Teddy came to me one day and informed me that he and Teresa had split up. He didn't look particularly happy about it but he was quite adamant that he didn't want to discuss it. I had grown very fond indeed of Teresa and although I was terribly disappointed, I didn't push the matter. I daresay I would know what had gone wrong at some point in the future.

Teddy accepted a job that was to take him away as far as the West Country.

"Don't worry Mum," he said, "It's not forever."
The job was to last approximately six months. So off he went with his suitcase and money in his pocket and a promise to keep in touch. As a Mother I found the experience of Teddy moving out of the family home quite a wrench, but I shouldn't have let it bother me because following a letter to him from Teresa, he phoned me to say he was on his way home. As he had only been gone a few weeks, my Mother's intuition was to kick in, and I found myself worried and anxiously awaiting his arrival.

On the evening prior to Teddy's expected arrival, I received several visitors. Namely, Teresa, her sister, two brothers and last but not least, Teresa's Mum. I invited them in and after giving Teresa my usual hug of welcome, I turned to her family and asked,

"Is there a problem?"

Teresa's older sister, it seemed was to be spokeswoman.

"I'm afraid there is," she replied. "Teresa is pregnant and we would like to know what you intend to do about it"

There was a moment's silence. Then I looked at Teresa and she nodded in confirmation. I turned to face the members of her family who were quietly and calmly awaiting my reply. There had not been the opportunity in the past year for us to be introduced; therefore I felt I should handle the situation with as much tact as possible.

First of all, I told them that no matter how things evolved between Teddy and Teresa, I would take on the responsibility along with my son to ensure that Teresa's financial needs would be taken care of and that I personally would stand by her and see her through to the end. After all, she was carrying my grandchild and the affection I had for Teresa was enough in itself to warrant my complete support. I told them of Teddy's expected arrival on the next day and pleaded with them to go home and allow these two young people the chance to at least discuss their problem together, alone.

"But," I declared, "I wish it known that no way is there going to be anything that would resemble a shot-gun wedding arranged at my home."

They left as quietly as they had arrived and no way did I feel put out by their visit. After all they were only being supportive and were quite obviously very concerned about Teresa and her expected baby's future.

Teresa looked at me and asked what she should do when she saw Teddy the next day.

"I'll give you the best advice I can," but it's up to you my darling, whether you follow it or not."

She must have had great trust in me because she followed my advice to the letter.

"You must offer him his freedom. Tell him he doesn't have to stay with you just because you are pregnant. It must be because he cares enough for you, yourself."

"Supposing he takes the offer of a way out," she cried.

"If he doesn't love you Teresa but marries you anyway, every time you have cross words pass between you its possible that the fact that he had to marry you could forever be thrown into your disputes, and your future together could end up in despair."
Both Teresa and I anxiously awaited Teddy's arrival.

Ted, it seemed had already guessed what the problem was even before I spoke to him. He was quite happy, he said, to leave it to us girls to resolve the problem one way or another.

Teddy arrived late afternoon, looking healthy and tanned. Outside work obviously agreed with him, and although he had been gone only a few weeks, I had missed him terribly. I informed him that Teresa would be arriving soon. After I'd fed and watered him, he dashed upstairs to take a bath.

Meanwhile, Teresa arrived looking very pretty and slightly flushed. I ushered her into the sitting room, and sat with her chatting away while we waited for Teddy. As soon as he came into the room, I left them alone, and made my way back to the kitchen to do the washing up; a difficult task when you're trying to keep your fingers crossed on both hands.

Sometime later they both confronted me with smiles on their faces that told me without the addition of words that all was going to be well.

The date for their wedding was set, and Ted and I promised to provide a wedding reception. Teresa's parents were very supportive as well. It was a very busy time for everyone. It was important to have this wedding before Teresa got too big. They found a flat, and although at first it was sparsely furnished, Teresa was able to make it look very homely.

The wedding went off without a hitch, and although the wedding photos showed quite clearly that Teresa was pregnant, it was obvious that it caused her no real problem. The reception started out by creating a split. Teresa's family and friends, mostly Irish, were all seated down one side of the room, while mine were huddled together on the opposite side.

"This won't do at all," I confided in my Dad.

"Don't worry daughter," he said. "Just wait awhile until everyone has downed a few drinks; you will see the difference."
I'm happy to say he was quite right. A wonderful time was had by all. Teddy and Teresa seemed quite happy with their lot, considering their unsettling start to their life together.

Four months on, Teresa gave birth to a beautiful baby girl and proved to be a good wife and Mother. Teddy played his part. He was a hard working young man. I can't recall him ever being out of work.

He very quickly built a name for himself within the family, as "Mr Know it all". And in truth, he was very knowledgeable and streetwise. Many people including family members would seek out his advice on various matters.

I remember the time he dared to take the police to the small claims court - something about the tyres on his vehicle. He won the day, but he paid the price; he was certain that every cop in the town had his registration number. In the end, in desperation, he exchanged the vehicle and donned a flat cap, and eventually the situation was resolved. Teddy realised that to take the police to court again for harassment would cause him more hassle than he was prepared to endure.

Teddy has always been a hard man to get the better of, but he's always ready to help the under dog. He loves children and animals and has given much of himself in these two areas. His best pal was an Alsatian named Benji. I bought him a brass plaque that he proudly nailed into the front garden wall that read "Never mind the dog, beware of the owner". Teddy was always ready to fight for his rights and often did. When Benji died of old age, Teddy felt the loss very deeply.

Approximately two years after the birth of their daughter, their son Tony was born. As they were growing up it was very noticeable that they were quite different in temperament. Whilst Tanya was bubbly, chatty and very outgoing, Tony was quiet and laid back, but they both developed to be very streetwise. It's always been my opinion that that was mostly down to Teddy's teachings.

He had travelled about quite a lot so there was much that he could teach his children. For a couple of years Teddy worked in the Middle East and parts of Africa. He took a job in a Sugar Refinery in the Sudan and this was for a big company that paid him extremely well. He worked in America for several months, and whilst there was involved in a car accident. He attended hospital as an outpatient at the same time as John Wayne, the film star was admitted and was to undergo treatment for Cancer. Teddy and my father both were ardent fans of this man. Teddy stated he would have given almost anything to meet him, but not this way. Although Teddy would spend many months at a time away from home, he would have wonderful tales to tell on his return visits home. Whether these long breaks working away was to be in part responsible or not, Teddy and Teresa's marriage was to travel down a very bumpy road. Of course they had their good times, and their union lasted approximately twenty-five years, but eventually with broken vows on both sides, the end came. Their separation and divorce was to prove to be a very angry and painful affair. I was devastated and felt there was little I could do but just be there for them. Thankfully, Tanya and Tony were at this time in their twenties. I found myself often having to console and counsel Tanya. It's true to say they both found themselves in the middle of mini war zone.

Teddy settled his affairs, and made preparations for a life in Australia. A dream he had nurtured for many years. At this time of writing, he has been there for three years. He has visited us all twice, and both Tanya and Tony have been able to spend time out there with him.

Teddy in America

He has tried several times to get me to visit, but I have a terror of flying, so I live in hope that one day he will come knocking on my door again; I feel sure he will. He phones me regularly and recently informed me that at last he had made it. He was now a legal Australian. He has a job that involves him in the building of boats - large catamarans that when launched leave him with a great sense of satisfaction. This work is so very different to the building trade when he lived in England.

Teddy with his own brand of charm, intelligence, and basic need to do the job right had worked his way up in the building trade and he eventually had gone into the business for himself.

It's true to say he can turn his hand to almost anything. So, I was not in the least surprised when he told me that he was now working with boats for a small family business. I could never look at Teddy without seeing my father. Teddy enjoyed a very close relationship with my Dad. When Dad died, Teddy held his emotions locked in, but after the funeral he was to shut himself away in his bedroom for some considerable time. Whatever went on behind that closed door is known only to him. I often wonder what Dad would have said to him if he had still been alive when Teddy declared to one and all that he was leaving for Australia.

I miss Teddy so very much. My one consolation is that he seems now to be very happy and has made many new friends. What more could a Mother wish for her son. He is also enjoying a new and loving relationship and maybe one day I will meet her. Until then, may he continue to be happy and stay healthy and of course keep in touch with us here in good old England.

I have his photo on my bedside table and say goodnight to him before I settle down to sleep. Tomorrow I plan to select a birthday card and I must remember to send it a week earlier; thereby ensuring he receives it in good time. I've also written him a poem, which I will enclose in the card. I can well imagine the grin on his face when he reads it, and I'm pretty sure I know what he will say.
     "Nice one Mum."
Good night my son until we talk to each other again, and I can tell you yet again how much I love you.

CHAPTER TWENTY

My Son Garry

Music is enjoyed by most people from all different cultures. It's difficult to imagine life without it. Then we have those who have a deep rooted need to play and create music and find in themselves a dedication that grows with them, and seems to touch at their very soul. This I am certain is what happened to Garry.

To watch his talent and his dedication grow, never seeming to falter at any stage of his life has always filled me with much pride and pleasure. It's difficult to put into words that would express fully how I feel. Even as a small child he would take my saucepans out of the cupboard, turn them upside down and bang away with a wooden spoon to his hearts content. He was always humming quietly to himself; he would hum himself to sleep - sometimes to the annoyance of his brother Teddy. Cleaning his teeth could turn into a musical event. Bath times often found us singing a duet together.

He was only seven years old when he first saw and heard the Violin. He must have been more than a little interested in having one because it was the one and only time that I can recall him ever coming close to demanding anything. I believe his exact words were, "Mum, I must have one". His school at that time had four Violins, and I'm happy to say that Ted and I were able to purchase one for him. He never needed to be pushed or even encouraged to practice. All his efforts came from within himself. Ted and I were both supportive, but what Garry has achieved regarding his musical talents is truly all his own.

At the age of ten his pride in his Violin was evident by the constant cleaning and polishing that was bestowed on that instrument. It's true to say there were times he would call out to me and say, "Mum, I'm going out to play football today". This somehow pleased me; I must admit to sometimes feeling concerned about the amount of time he spent behind a closed door. Garry, at this age was even showing signs of knowing exactly what he wanted out of life. He was never demanding, and whilst his two brothers at times created waves, Garry's were mere ripples.

At the age of eleven, I was able to get Garry a place at the Grove School, which at that time had a very impressive youth Orchestra. He went from strength to strength. I remember the first time he played solo at one of the school's many concerts. Parents and friends were invited to attend. I sat, hanging on to every single note he played, willing him to get through to the end without dropping a note. And of course, he came through with flying colours.

In the early stages, I remember sitting in a little waiting room while Garry took his violin exams. These are stressful times for young people and I didn't do so well myself. He would come out through the door with a grin on his face that said it all. As he got older he would quite happily go it alone.

The school Orchestra grew in strength, leading to a musical performance to be held at our local White Rock Theatre. Many schools were to participate in this big event. A woman by the name of Mrs Blackwell who was Head of Music in the Hastings area was to play an important part in putting this show together. These evenings of music by local young musicians proved to be very entertaining and very importantly a firm basis for these young people to express themselves, and build up their confidences.

I remember the occasion when I was introduced to Mrs Blackwell. She shook my hand very warmly and proceeded to confide in me that many young people learn to play the violin but only a few become violinists. She told me if Garry was to continue with his music studies he could become a violinist. I felt so very proud of him that evening. Garry always managed to stay very modest about it all. He often had to put up with being teased by his schoolmates, but he never ever allowed this treatment to affect the way he felt about his violin. If he did, he never allowed it to show.

When he left school at sixteen he had earned for himself six "O" level qualifications and one "A" level, the "A" being for music of course. He decided to take a year off. There was no lazing around for him; he set about earning some money. For a while he went hop picking, but then managed to get himself a job working in the office of a Solicitor named Perring.

At seventeen, he was offered a place at Lewis Music College. He was there for two years. I'm happy to say he always found his way home on seasonal breaks. To earn money on these breaks, he mostly worked on the buses as a bus conductor. This introduction to the general public left Garry unimpressed to say the least; mostly the lack of please and thank you, mannerisms that he was brought up to believe was the norm. He decided to treat these people in kind.

The next stage in Garry's young life was to take him further away, as far as Dartington in Devon, situated far west of our own town of Hastings. But fortunately Garry was still able to travel home and spend most breaks with us. He had also saved enough money to purchase a second-hand 70cc Honda Moped which he rode all the way to Dartington College on his very first trip there; this was to take 14 hours. So it's easy to understand that after that he decided to travel by train along with his bike.

Dartington College of Music was to give Garry two years of learning that I'm certain added further building blocks to his talents. Learning to play the piano and to write music was just two of those building blocks. Unfortunately at some point in those two years, Garry walked out of the piano lessons. It seemed he did not have a very good rapport with his piano teacher - which is true to say, is a first for Garry, but thankfully he was to resume his piano playing at a later date in his life, and this was to stand him in good stead when he began to compose his own music.

To help with the financial side of things, Garry was to share digs with two young budding musicians from his own hometown. He had been friends with them for years and of course they shared a common interest, that being their music. These two friends were females and very much as sisters to Garry.

So a genuinely felt need to look out for them both stayed with Garry during this period of his life, especially as their parents had proclaimed how happy they were that Garry would be part of their existence. This I felt left Garry feeling greatly responsible for their safety and well-being. No real task for him I'm sure, as he was quite fond of them. He confided to me that at least there was a chance he'd get his cooking and ironing done. He was in for a big surprise.

Neither of the girls could cook. A call from the kitchen area asking Garry how to cook peas was a strong indication that he would be likely to spend much time in the kitchen himself. Although I had taught him only the very basic side of preparing a meal, it proved to be much more than the girls could cope with. Garry's cooking skills improved with time; he really had no choice if he was to keep hunger pangs at bay. He learnt to cook a very mean Spaghetti Bolognese.

On one occasion when he was running late, he asked one of the girls to press his jeans. This too proved to be a big mistake. She pressed them flat, which left him wearing them with sharp seams on the outside rather than at the centre, which was the fashion then. I wondered at the time if this was female logic at work. But, nevertheless it proved to be a happy and workable arrangement for the three of them.

With his time at Dartington College now over, he arrived home a little sooner than expected.

"I hope your not going to be disappointed Mum" he declared, "but I have to tell you that I was offered a place in a London Orchestra in the second strings section, but I turned it down. I just can't see myself playing in an Orchestral Pit, not now, not ever."

"Well" I replied, "if not classical music, what are you planning for yourself?"

"It's my intention to play Folk music," he said.

And that is exactly what he did do.

Garry has never been content to allow his talent to become stagnant. He's always eagerly tried new ideas, but whatever he's achieved musically, his classical training has been the very basis of it all.

Garry has travelled extensively but never to my knowledge on his own. Usually it was with a small group of three or four young talented musicians. His violin case eventually became covered in stick on labels from so many different countries, I completely lost track.

Money was scarce for them all, but they thoroughly enjoyed busking, which was a source of acquiring money, given generously by the general public, in exchange for their musical talents.
In between these adventurous trips he acquired a job as a Carpet Fitter's Mate, and much to my horror became a very competent fitter himself. This is a job that requires the use of very sharp small knife, and as he was to earn his living for a number of years fitting carpets, I am amazed that he got away with no more than one small scar. This surely should never have been a choice of work for a violinist. He always assured me that he took great care. It's true to say he had been well trained by a professional man.

Garry, now in his twenties, meets and marries a young woman named Gail Toogood, but it wasn't too many years before the stress and strain on both sides of this relationship began to build up and the eventual split came, followed by a divorce.

There were two very young children to be considered here, and I showed my support through them. Thomas, the eldest and his brother, Edward came through it all unscarred, and I believe it was down to the fact that their parents both behaved in a mature and intelligent fashion. Neither were to use the children or to place them in a tug of war situation.

I had babysat the boys from when they were only a few months old - Monday to Friday, and even after the separation of Garry and Gail, I continued to do the same. It was always a pleasure for me; I never ever saw it as a chore. Gail had a very good job that promised her a secure future. She made the most of her children's evenings and weekends. After the separation, Garry had no choice but to come home to me. He had left the house and contents to Gail to secure the future of his children.

As time passed, the boys became quite used to having two homes and I think its true to say they both did well out of it all. Garry put much more than his fair share into the household expenses while living with me; taking into account that the boys both had very good appetites.

Garry's musical bookings were bringing him closer to being able to go professional. Which meant he would be able to put Carpet Fitting and that sharp knife behind him forever. This was brought about by his teaming up with a guitarist named Pete Fyfe. They called themselves "Band of Two". This duo was to be Garry's main source of income for many years. The friendship that sprang up between them remains steadfast to this very day.

Around about the same time a band was put together and was to give years of fantastic music. There were six members in all, and they called this band "Better Days". My sitting room became "The Music Room". At times Garry would by necessity ask to use this room for group practice. Fortunately my immediate neighbour's son was a drummer, and so this insured a certain tolerance by both households. On these occasions, I would declare music ceased at 10.00pm, at which point I would serve up tea and sandwiches. From that time on, I was known and addressed as "Garry's Mum".

Garry was now writing music in earnest and developing his vocal chords. He was also taking quite an interest in teaching himself to play the guitar. He met a young man named Roger Flack and together they set about forming a band. They got together with some very talented young musicians. After many practice sessions, Garry and Roger decided the time was right to launch this band out onto the music circuit. It proved to be a great success. Garry has been a part of many bands and group venues. His talent as a violinist was often called upon to participate in their creating of tapes, and then discs, that no doubt are still circulating out there to this very day.

But this band that was put together by himself and Roger was to be their baby, and it was with much pride on their first public performance that they announced themselves as "The Tabs".

A young woman was to enter Garry's life at a time when I believe he was neither needing nor looking for love. She was petite with long dark hair and beautiful eyes, and her name was Rosie. Eventually they moved into a flat together, thus giving his sons Tom and Eddy yet another place to call home. Rosie being of such a sweet nature won the boys affection very quickly.

Band of Two.
Consisting of Pete Fyfe [left] and my son Garry [right].

Rose is poetic and artistic in her own right and loves music. So its there for all to see how very compatible these two are. Eventually they moved into a three-bedroom house. It came as no real surprise when they announced to one and all that they were going to get married. Garry made a point of telling his sons first and admitted to me he was just a little concerned how they would take this news. He need not have worried; the boys had had two years in which to get to know Rose, and were absolutely delighted.

At this moment in time, Garry and Rose are both extremely happy and quite obviously in love. It's my sincere belief they will share many blissful moments. What could possibly please a Mother more than to know her son is happy and well, and very content with his lot. He may not have become a big international star in his musical career, but he has definitely had his moments. He has earned the admiration and respect of his fellow musicians and has many ardent fans. Life for Garry at this time finds him still pushing his limits musically and enjoying the knowledge and satisfaction of his many achievements. He has numerous tapes and discs to his credit and I find myself often sitting and quietly listening to and drinking in the various forms of his efforts. He has just completed a tour of "Feast of Fiddles". I had the pleasure of attending a performance held in Chatham. I found myself still buzzing on the following day from its impact on my senses.

Garry is a well-balanced individual, though it's true to say he does not suffer fools gladly. At this stage in his life, he can be found enjoying a quiet contentment that can only come from a soul that is at peace with himself and what he has achieved.

He is surrounded by love, and he gives of himself without question to those he cares about. Mum, he says to me, if you need me, you only have to call. I love him dearly and my wish for him is that the contentment and peace of mind that blesses him now stays with him for the duration of his life.

CHAPTER TWENTY-ONE

Ted and I

Its time now for me to take you back to the time when I brought my son Darran home from the Nursing Home to find Mother ill once more.

Although my marriage was still showing strong indications of strain, Darran was to bring to Ted and I a joy beyond belief. He was such a beautiful child and we both loved him very much. Ted saw him as a chance to make good any mistakes he believed he had made with Darran's two older brothers; his words not mine.

Speaking for myself, Darran was a miracle of life that I had experienced for the third time. There was no doubt in my mind; I was definitely meant to be a Mother.

Ted was a good husband and father. His jealousy and possessiveness in the early years was very flattering, but as time went by I felt that I had done everything possible to earn his trust. When questioned Ted would claim that he trusted me completely. The problem for him it seems went back as far as his childhood. Everything he had ever loved or valued was at some point in his life taken away from him and had left him, I felt, with many insecurities. I loved him very much, but I was too young and inexperienced to deal with it in a knowledgeable way. I felt certain that time and love would conquer all.

My life with Ted was a good one. After all, I had everything that I had ever wanted - a man who loved me, a home of my own and not least my children. The next couple of years were pretty stable. Darran did indeed have a positive influence on both Ted and myself, and occasionally we would enjoy some very light hearted and amusing situations. I always kept a small plastic blue tennis racket in the kitchen to ward off flies, wasps and the like and if a fly for example found its way into the house, I would grab the bat and race around the house chasing it with a determination that always had everyone smiling. It even led some people to believe that I was just a little cranky.

One bright and sunny day, Ted was busying himself at the sink when a wasp with its unmistakable buzz found its way into the kitchen. I grabbed the bat, poised, and waited to take my shot. Ted quietly told me to leave it alone and tried to assure me it would fly straight back out through the door from where it had entered.

"You will only get somebody stung," he warned me.

Well, never a truer word said. I took aim and caught the wasp in full flight. My aim was intended towards the kitchen door. It all happened so quickly, the wasp went up in the air and came straight down and disappeared down the front of Ted's shirt. As I watched him slapping himself about and finally ripping off his shirt, I just took to my heels and ran. After two or three minutes I crept back to the house and called out.

"Can I come back in now?" to which Ted replied with a grudging "Yes".

I truly was so sorry. The wasp had stung him twice. Ever after that if I was seen grabbing for the blue bat, everyone immediately vacated the area.

Then there was the occasion when Ted brought home a black and white stray dog. He knew my fear of dogs; so in all honesty, I felt more than a little cross with him. He managed to win me round when he told me that the railway management had decided that the dog would have to be put down because not only was it a nuisance, but a danger as well. A Railway Station was not an ideal home for a dog. The men including Ted had regularly fed it, so therefore the Station Goods Yard and the rail tracks became a regular haunt for this wondering and lost animal. Ted named this dog Sam, and I believe he had become very fond of him and had decided to risk my wrath and bring him home.

Sam was given a good bath and brushed until his coat shone. Ted promised me he would take Sam to the vets the next day and get him checked out. The next morning Ted left home for his early morning shift. When Darran and myself arose from bed some two hours later, we made our way downstairs to the kitchen. I gently opened the kitchen door and peeped in. Sam immediately let out a growl, and then proceeded to bark. I quickly closed the door, retreated back along the hall and sat down with Darran on the bottom stair. Darran was too young at that time to understand fully what was going on, and I was very aware of not wanting to pass my fears onto him. We sat there for about five minutes, and realising I couldn't sit on the stairs until three o'clock when Ted's shift would be over, I decided to make another attempt to get into the kitchen. I opened the door and this time called out "Sam, Sam, Good boy". But Sam had positioned himself directly behind the door and let out such a torrent of barking that I'm sure my heart missed several beats. That crafty streetwise animal had been there with both ears cocked just waiting for me to make my move.

Now I'm back sitting on the bottom stair. Fortunately, the phone was in the hall. I picked it up and dialled Ted's work number. In all the years that he had worked on the railways I had never until now done such a thing.

"Is it an emergency?" a voice asked.

"Yes, it most certainly is," I replied.

"Please hold the line madam." Seven minutes later I heard Ted's voice on the line.

"What's up love?"

"You're blinkin' Sam," I replied "won't let Darran and I in the kitchen, and I refuse to sit here for seven hours waiting for you to come home!"

"I'll be there in twenty-five minutes," he said, and then the line went dead.

Ted arrived home to a wonderful welcome from Sam, and once again talked me into allowing the dog to get to know us all. Ted insisted that I should feed Sam, which he assured me would create a strong bond. Yes, I thought to myself, if I don't lose a hand in the process.

The Vet did not have good news for Ted. Whilst he gave Sam a clean bill of health, he proclaimed that Sam had been running wild for some considerable time and would at the first opportunity run for it; Sam's paws told all.

Well in time he was proved right; Sam did indeed leg it, but we did manage to hang onto him for a few months. We honestly thought we had won him over, so allowed him access to the back garden. Big mistake. He dug his way out and was again running free. I told myself that Sam had enjoyed his time with us, but for Sam enough was enough. Ted spent weeks searching for him, but to no avail.

I had grown very fond of Sam but decided not to inform Ted of this fact, just in case it would encourage him to bring home yet another dog. I was very aware of the importance of allowing children to have pets, and teaching them to care for and respect animals. At various times there was a tortoise, rabbits, hamsters and a tank of fish. I must be honest and say that my level of hygiene made it difficult to have animals in the home, but I did my best by the children.

As a child myself, I did not approve of Zoo's. To see large animals pacing up and down in a cage distressed me terribly. But nothing gives me greater pleasure now than to watch television programmes that show the wildlife series, especially the big cats. Animals in their natural surroundings can teach us humans a lot about the code of life and living behaviour.

Darran at this time was four years old, and unfortunately the stress and strain between Ted and myself was very evident yet again. The next two years was to be a very trying and unhappy time for us both. Thankfully there were happy times to be enjoyed as well, but usually our time was centred around Darran.

Mum would talk to me and offer advise, none of which could be put into practice because I could never get Ted to sit and talk to me. So I would ask her how could Ted and I resolve anything if he constantly clammed up and refused to discuss our problems? The inevitable happened, and I suffered a nervous breakdown. Three days of my life simply disappeared. I went to my sister Mary's home. She put me to bed and phoned for the doctor. When he saw the state I was in he gave me an injection that was to completely knock me out, and returned again the following two days and administered the same treatment. At this time I was aware of only two things. The first being that I was in a bed at Mary's home and the second that Mary was sitting on my bed just gently tapping my thigh. Strange as it may seem this was to have a very soothing effect on me. My doctor informed me that I had actually told him off for taking so long to answer my call for help. He claimed that he had in fact responded very quickly. Obviously time had lost all meaning for me. I was to stay in Mary's care for a week, at which time I refused to see anybody, even my children. Not wanting to see my children was so alien to me as a person that it was to leave me feeling a guilt that stayed with me for a very long time.

I was to find myself on my return home very subdued, and it was several weeks before I felt anything like human. Ted did his best to help me, but the problems that were tearing us apart unfortunately were still there.

In my effort to get Ted to talk I even went on a hunger strike. This lasted three days. I had told Ted of my intentions, but it was Mum that eventually pleaded with him to sit down and talk our problems through. I suggested that we both seek some counselling, but Ted being a very private person, declined empathetically. I personally believe this proved to be a big mistake.

At a time when we had both reached the end of our endurance, a time when I was still recovering from my nervous breakdown and Ted was so close to having a breakdown himself, everything was to hit rock bottom. Ted did the unbelievable; he struck me. This action of his devastated the both of us. Never in all the years that we had been together had such a thing happened. Ted was so distressed, that

I pleaded with him to forgive himself. This was when he agreed to take counselling with me.

We kept many visits with a Mr Bott. He was to convince me that although I had said all the right things to Ted, our split was inevitable. Loyalty between Ted and I was never questioned by either of us, but I think it's fair to say that I had changed. Now the children were all grown up I wanted Ted and I to socialise a little; I was no longer the little girl in his life, but a fully mature woman and this I believe set off his possessiveness to new heights. He always used to say to me that someone one day would take me away from him. In the twenty-five years we were together this never happened. It was very unfortunate that our son Garry walked into the house immediately after this unpleasant event and was to quietly say to his father,

"Don't you think Dad that its time that you left?"

The making of that statement, I believe, has stayed with Garry, and he once was quoted as saying that perhaps his Dad had not forgiven him for it.

So it was that Ted left and made his home in Oxford. He made regular visits to see Darran who was only six years old at this time. I always made it very easy for Ted to see him. Our divorce finale on the 6th September 1979 was to mark the end of our marriage and place a new set of crossroads for the both of us. It was a painful time for me, and a time of uncertainty for Darran. It was at least three years before I could get on with my life. Ted was to set up home with a new lady in his life, who he eventually married. This was to give me an incentive to really move on with my life. Ted and I managed to stay friendly through it all; we have a mutual respect for each other, and stay in touch. Our sons and our grandchildren have always managed to keep in touch with him and visa versa. Ted was always a good husband and father, and I can honestly say that for me there are no regrets and I would like to think he feels the same.

CHAPTER TWENTY-TWO

My Son Darran

Darran was born in troubled times but the love that Ted and I both had for him I firmly believe was the strong and guiding light that was to stand him in good stead.

In the first six years of his life while Ted and I were still together, there stands out one or two memorable occasions.

My Mum was living with us then and she would indulge Darran as only a Nan can, and whilst I saw no real harm in this, I would on occasion warn her that it could bounce back at her. When he reached the age of four years, I decided to start giving Darran pocket money. There were four family members at home at that time; Ted, myself, Mum and Garry, and it was agreed that we would each give Darran two shillings each, making in total eight shillings - this being in the time of old money, just before the decimal system was introduced. He was able to buy his weekly comic, and the occasional bag of sweets. Ted and I started a bank account for him with a small deposit. Because it was a junior account, our local bank at the time was handing out moneyboxes free of charge. This moneybox had a big round orange coloured face with black facial markings and a mass of black hair; it also had two protruding front feet. Darran was encouraged to save just a little of his new found pocket full of wealth, and he nicknamed his moneybox the 'Diddy Man'. Darran was to experience that bad behaviour could result in his losing his pocket money. He had been very rude to his Nan, so I told him that Nanny would not be giving him his two shillings that week. So came Saturday morning, Darran did his usual round collecting his pocket money. I had already reminded Mum that on no account was she to undermine my discipline by giving Darran her two shillings.
  "Of course I won't darling," she assured me.
I was upstairs making the beds up, when Darran asked please could he have his pocket money. I reached for my purse and I dropped a

two-shilling piece into his hand. I noticed that he was holding his usual amount. I looked at his face and he gave me such a sweet innocent smile. I grabbed him and marched him downstairs to my Mother who also had a sweet smile on her face.

"Mother!" I declared, "How could you?"

"I had to give it to him," she said

"What do you mean by you had to give it to him?"

"He threatened to kick my gammy leg if I didn't!"

"This, Mother," I said "comes from your spoiling him."

Then I turned to Darran and assured him that not only would he give Nanny back her two shilling piece, but he wouldn't get one from her come the following Saturday.

Darran learnt this lesson well because it was never repeated. Unbeknown to him we all sat and had a good laugh about it, although I was certainly not amused at the time.

I was never one for entering my babies into competitions, but Ted and I did take many photos of them. I had just come back from having Darran's hair cut and styled and he was looking particularly smart. Ted declared that it called for a studio photograph to be done. This was a rarity for us as money was not to be spent frivolously. So off I went unaware that the photo could automatically be entered into a competition. So imagine my confusion when neighbours were calling out to me across the street "congratulations!" Eventually I was to ask why I was being congratulated, only to be told Darran had won first prize in the four to six year old section, and that his photo was in the local newspaper, "The Observer". I must admit to having felt very proud.

It's strange that some of the things you remember can be the silliest. Darran was still four years old when he took to his heart a little Gnome that was red and green in colour, and had come into his possession stuck on the end of a pencil. He discarded the pencil and would carry this Gnome, which was small enough to fit into the palm of his hand. He carried it everywhere; even placed it on his bedside table at night and sometimes under his pillow. Darran on one occasion was having a slight tantrum about having to go to bed. Ted spotted the red and green Gnome and popped it into his pocket. Darran eventually gave up trying to find it and made his way to bed, with a promise from his Dad that if he were to be a very good boy, the Gnome would find his way back.

"He's probably left you," Ted told him, "because you were naughty".

Young Darran

After two days had passed and Darran proved what a good boy he was, Ted placed the Gnome somewhere in the room, and we sat back and waited for Darran to spot it. When he did he grabbed it up and placed it tightly in his fist and ran to and fro Ted and myself crying out with glee "he's back, he's back, he's back!"

The Gnome would only disappear if Darran had been naughty. This little game was to continue on and off for about two years. Ted took great care that the game did not distress Darran. Darran was always convinced the Gnome would come back because his Daddy said it would. I still have it in my possession to this very day.

At six years and six months old, Darran was to experience his father leaving home. Although he was to see his father every weekend, it did not save him from feelings of hurt and confusion. I counselled him constantly. When retiring to bed myself I would look in on him only to often find him crying. I would soothe and stay with him until he fell asleep. In the mornings I would find him curled up into my back because at some time in the night he had crept quietly into my bed. I was advised to discourage this behaviour but found I could not. I still believe that I did the right thing because eventually little by little Darran made the transition to his own bed all by himself.

A very strong bond was to grow between Darran and myself. I was to go to great lengths to assure him that his relationship with his Mum and Dad was secure, with weekly visits from his Dad, especially in Darran's tender years. Ted never ever let his son down, even though it was approximately a hundred and twenty miles from Oxford to Hastings. Ted was to make the journey without fail.

With all this tender loving care, it did not prevent Darran from occasionally showing his disapproval by putting me in a position of having to show and prove my loyalty to him. I'd left him playing in the sitting room while I went about my household chores.

He came and found me and held my hand and proceeded to lead me into the sitting room and declared that there was something he wanted to show me. My smoky glass coffee table was covered completely with candle wax. I just stood there completely speechless.

"Are you going to smack me?" Darran asked.

"No," I replied, "But I'm sorry to have to tell you this, but you are going to clean it all off, and there will be no tea for you until the job is done."

I gave him a cloth and left him there. Fifteen minutes later I peeped into the room to find him on his knees rubbing away, and tears flowing down his cheeks. He had only managed to clean a small corner. My heart melted and, armed with a cloth of my own, I entered the sitting room, sunk to my knees beside him and proceeded to help him clean it all off. It proved to be a most difficult task, one that I'm sure Darran at the age of six would never have been able to complete on his own. We eventually enjoyed a hearty tea, and then both sat with our arms around each other, squashed up in one armchair to watch some television until it was time for his bath and then bed.

Darran was now seven years old and Ted, Darran and myself had settled down to a comfortable routine of tolerance and acceptance, but still with the occasional act of defiance from Darran.

I'd gotten into the habit of allowing Darran to have two or three playmates to join him in our back garden. At this stage I was not prepared to allow him to play out in the street. At teatime I'd see the children back into their own homes and bring Darran in for the usual clean up before sitting down at the table for tea. He had begun to display what I can only term as tantrums. He was making it quite clear to me that the idea of having his friends sent home and breaking up his playtime met with his disapproval, in a display of jumping up and down on the spot. The task of cleaning him up so we could have tea was proving to be a nightmare. One evening I decided this had to stop, and called upon myself to use a firmer hand. One good slap on the back of his leg got his immediate attention. Once he recovered from the shock, being the first time I had ever put my hand to him, he ran down the length of the hallway and turned to face me and cried out, "I will tell Daddy what you did when he comes on Saturday!" I slowly and calmly walked towards him, turned him around and delivered one slap on the back of the other leg, and told him to tell his Daddy about that one as well.

At a later date I checked with Ted if Darran had in fact mentioned this incident.

"Not a word," replied Ted.
I felt a stab of pride for my son - the fact that he hadn't taken the opportunity to run tales. The occasion never arose again for me to take him to task regarding tantrums.

The love between my Mum and Darran was to become very strong and deep rooted. She was always there to give comfort and advice to him whenever he needed it. Darran was able to soak up love and affection like a sponge, and give the same in return.

Mum would often complain of backache and Darran would sit on the arm of her chair and gently massage her back to help soothe away her pain. They both had their little secrets that they would confide in with each other, even at times sharing a little playful joke at my expense.

The three of us would find much comfort in each other. We each were nursing emotional stresses that served as a kind of bond that bound us together.

Life was to continue in this way. Dad still made his twice-weekly visits, whilst all the time Mum continued to need more and more care to be taken of her.

Darran at the age of eleven was now able to make visits to his Dad. I'd put him on a coach that would take him to a designated point and Ted would be there to meet him, and then they would travel onto Oxford together. This would enable Darran to stay with his Dad for quite long breaks. Mum and I missed him terribly but these times spent with his Dad proved to be very good for both Ted and Darran. On his return trips, I'd be at the coach station to meet him. Usually he would be laden with small gifts, new clothes on his back, and a smile on his face that could challenge the glow of the sun itself.

There were still times when I could experience a bad hair day, and Darran could have the occasional bad school day. One time stands out in my mind. When questioning him about his behaviour, I asked him, "Darran, why are you behaving like this?" to which he replied,

"It's probably because I come from a one parent family". I just stared at him for a moment, trying to collect my thoughts.

"Well, that would be me my son, because this is where you live".

I quietly informed him that he had just denied his father, and he should go to his room and think on what he had said. Ten minutes later he came down stairs, and slowly approached me, and said, "Mum, I'm sorry. I don't want to deny my father".

"Of course you don't darling. Let's forget all about it, and we will never speak of it again".

And we never did.

It was now time for Darran to move on to secondary schooling. It was also a time of change in the educational system. Grammar Schools were now out of favour, and were to be replaced by Secondary Modern.

William Parker was one such Grammar school, but unfortunately could not be my choice for Darran because I lived just outside of the appointed area. But Darran was to bring home a letter from his teacher on his last day before breaking up for the school holidays stating that if any parent felt they had just cause for a place to be offered for their child, they should apply in writing to the local Education Authority. This I did, and received in reply a time and place to plead my case. At the appointed time, I found myself sitting in a waiting room along with several other parents. I glanced at my watch and realised they were running quite late. Eventually my name was called and in I walked. In front of me was a high platform on which stood a large wooden desk, and at this desk sat four people: three gentlemen, and one lady, with them all looking down at me. I decided I was not going to feel intimidated.

There was just one spokesman, and he decided to proceed by apologizing for the long delay, and claimed that the previous lady had gone on and on. I believe this was his way of letting me know it was time that we all went home for tea, thereby hoping I wouldn't feel inclined to take up too much time. I decided to make my plea on Darran's behalf short and directly to the point, soothing their frayed senses.

I stated that the divorce of his father and myself had been a traumatic experience for us all. But the efforts of both Darran's parents and the love we had given him, and our determination that he would not suffer because of it, called for the support of the Educational system, and if they were to decide in favour of a place for Darran at William Parker School, their offer would not be wasted.

"Please," I said, "Give my son the break he needs and deserves".

My speech lasted less than three minutes. I thanked them for their time and consideration, turned on my heel and left. A lady waiting her turn in the waiting room smiled at me and said, "Gosh, you were quick".

I went home and waited for the letter they claimed I would receive in due course letting me know of their decision.

When receiving confirmation that I had acquired a place for Darran, I was so delighted. Darran himself was eager to know what it was that I had said because many of his classmates parent's had applied but had been turned down. I didn't think it a very good idea for Darran to know, and perhaps discuss with his classmates, something that might cause unrest. So I just told him that it was information that was just for me to know, and for him to find out when I was good and ready to tell him. Darran had long since learnt that to argue with me would not bear fruit.

I was discussing with my neighbour the problem we were having with frogs. Both gardens were swamped with them. She did have a very small fishpond in her front garden, but we couldn't work out why all these frogs were treating it as home. Darran eventually confided to me that two years previously he had tipped a jar full of tadpoles into the small fishpond. So, of course they grew into frogs and returned every year to spawn. My neighbour was very fond of Darran, so all was forgiven.

Darran at the age of thirteen was to experience for the first time a death in the family. My Dad at the age of seventy-five died in February 1983 from Coronary Thrombosis. Darran was so taken up with dealing with his Mum and his Nan's grief that I'm not at all sure how the loss of his granddad affected him, although there was much affection that existed between the two. Darran was to tell us that he felt cheated because he had not spent much time at all with his granddad and now of course, he never would. This experience was to leave Darran with the knowledge that life itself could never be taken for granted, and it took all my patience to help him deal with the fact that at some point he would have to come to terms with losing his Nan.

In his first year at William Parker, Darran was subjected to a considerable amount of bullying.

"I'm not a coward Mum," he would say, "But I can't fight all of them."

I would plead with him to allow me to go to the school and have it sorted out.

"If you do that Mum, I will run away from school. The class will think I'm a sissy!"

It might have been more acceptable for his Dad to go but not his Mum. Unfortunately, Ted was in Oxford.

So it was, that Darran struggled through his first year, and there were many times that I would ask myself if I had made the right decision to get him sent to William Parker, instead of allowing him to go to the school that all his previous classmates had moved on to.

But come his second year, he had found the way to assert himself and was much happier. He was reprimanded on several occasions for interfering and trying to protect the new first year arrivals. The Headmaster confided in me that he admired what Darran had done but could not appear to condone these actions. I declared that I understood and even agreed with him. But when Darran was to witness bullying it always made him angry. It seemed that his own first year experiences were to always stay with him through his life.

Darran attending William Parker School

Darran's school reports were always acceptable standards. So, imagine my surprise when in his last year, I was called to the school for a chat with the Headmaster. He asked me if I was having any problems at home with Darran.

"Absolutely not," I rejected, and he proceeded to inform me that Darran was becoming somewhat troublesome for a couple of his teachers. My question for him was,

"Why these teachers and not the others, whom I had recently received good reports from?"

"A personality clash," he told me, which was not unusual in young males of fifteen and sixteen. He could see I was somewhat confused.

"The only explanation I can give you Mrs Blakeley," he said, "Is that there are teachers and there are teachers".

I promised to have words with my son, shook hands, and left.

Darran's response to me was simply he didn't like the way these two teachers spoke to him.

"If they show me respect," he said, "I will show them some".

Three months before it was time for Darran to be able to leave school, I made an appointment to see the Headmaster. I reminded him of my last visit and of the question he had asked me at that time, and my answer to him that 'No, I was not having problems at home with Darran'.

"Well," I said, dejectedly, "I'm here today to inform you that I am now having problems at home and that I will be keeping Darran away from school. I am to set him up with an apprenticeship with his older brother, and I am quite prepared to take on the powers that be in the process".

I felt that the school had let Darran down in his last year - not that I excused Darran of his behaviour because I certainly did not.

I was visited by a Truant Officer and advised that I was in fact breaking the law. I met with a Mr Morton-Hower to discuss Darran's problems and mine. He interviewed Darran and myself separately on behalf of the Local Education Authority. He asked me to visit an establishment that housed problem children. I did so; only to report back to him that there was no way I was going to sit Darran in a class full of delinquents. To my surprise, he was to agree with me completely stating that Darran was a very intelligent boy just going through a bad patch. He advised me to carry on the way I had been, and that he would slow down his legal papers, so that by the time these papers found their way through the system, Darran would be legally free to go out to work.

So it was that Garry took Darran on and proceeded to train him as a carpet fitter. This proved to be a hair-raising time for Garry. Darran was not an easy trainee. But Garry bless him, hung in there for four or five years and was to suffer a certain amount of mental bombardment.

During this time, Darran was to meet and fall in love with a young girl named Tracey. Despite warnings, Darran was to come and tell me that Tracey was pregnant. He was just sixteen in the May of that year. Holly, a baby girl, was born in the September of the same year. Tracey thankfully was one year older than Darran. I helped to find them a flat and between them they decorated it and made a very presentable home for themselves. Unfortunately, this relationship was doomed from the very beginning; they were both much too young. Tracey developed a breast abscess and was feeling unwell. Plus both Darran and Tracey were lacking in sleep due to baby Holly cutting teeth. I offered to sleep with Holly in their sitting room and did so for three nights running. This gave the young couple a chance to get some really good rest.

By the time Holly was just one year old, Tracey went home to her mother and Darran found his way back to me. He was left with quite a few household bills and I helped him to clear this all up. My sister Mary bought what furniture Tracey had left with him; this also helped him pay off the bills. Mary managed to eventually sell it all over a period of time. It was a very kind thing for her to do - that kind gesture is typical of my sister Mary.

Although Darran was given access through the legal system to be a father to Holly, Tracey was to be totally uncooperative and would not hand Holly over. After a year, Darran gave up. His own Solicitor told him there was nothing more that he could do. This was a very unhappy and miserable time for Darran. My distress was nothing in comparison with his. I had never felt so helpless in my entire life.

Darran loved his baby so very much; he was totally besotted with her. It was impossible for him to hide his suffering. I have never been able to understand how Tracey could have done such a terrible thing. I must confess that I have always considered myself to be a person incapable of hate, but this was a time that brought me the closest to such feelings that I have ever been.

Tracey now had a new man with her, and she wanted Darran completely out of her life. Darran's Solicitor told him that although Tracey was defying the courts, it had never been known for an uncooperative mother to be sent to prison. So therefore, after trying to reason with Holly's mother for more than a year, there was nowhere else for Darran to go. Although Darran was working at the age of seventeen, his level of earnings allowed him to claim 'legal aid'. But this now was to be withdrawn because in their opinion, Darran's case was hopeless. Many fathers are dealing with this problem still today. When will the law in this country bring about a solution to this heart-rending problem? Father's are capable of feelings of great love, and it is very important that their offspring should be able to tap into the source.

At eighteen, Darran was settling down and getting on with his life. He could still wrap his nan around his little finger. I walked into the kitchen to find Mum doing the washing up for me and at the same time trying to control a fit of giggles.

On asking Darran what was going on, he informed me that nan, in her eagerness to get the washing up done before I arrived, had grabbed Darran's plate of freshly cooked eggs, and to his utter amazement had plonked it straight into the washing up water. He wasn't able until a little later to see the funny side. I looked over Mum's shoulder to see two eggs sunny side up floating to the surface of the bubbly washing up water.

Darran – martial artist

**Darran dressed as a Roman soldier during the filming of
the movie Gladiator**

The death of my father had hit Mum very badly, and I believed at the time that his death had contributed to yet a further decline in her health.

She was now extremely ill, and the whole family including the grandchildren were extremely aware that the time for Mum to leave us was very near. So when it came you could think that all of us would have been more prepared and better able to deal with it. But the level of grief throughout the family was tremendous. I felt it very strange that Darran could not allow me to comfort him. He constantly shed tears, but no sound would ever pass his lips. We all know that time heals, but even so Darran would say many times that he would never come to terms with losing his nan. At the age of twenty-one, he was to put on a brave face for the outside world. Even now at this time of my writing, and Darran being the age of thirty-five, he can still become watery eyed when talking about his nan.

Darran would work out regularly at the local gym and was developing a physique that was attracting much attention from the opposite sex. He took up and became very serious about Martial Arts and this was to give Darran a sense of well being and rebuilt his confidence. He passed all his grades with distinction and very proudly wore his black belt.

When he needed to boost his income from Carpet Fitting, he would take on work as a Doorman and Bouncer. After eight years of this kind of hassle, where he found himself having to resort to dealing with considerable acts of violence, Darran decided he had had more than enough of this kind of life and was to try something that was totally different. He joined several agencies that were to find him work in the acting profession. He enjoyed this very much and was given work on the BBC's 'Eastenders' and ITV's 'The Bill'; just two popular shows on television at the time. He also did various telly adverts, and got a part of a roman soldier in the film 'Gladiator' which was a great thrill for him. In this kind of work he was to meet many famous people; to name a few there was the film director

Steven Spielberg and stars Richard Harris, Michael Caine, Russell Crowe, Dame Judy Dench and many more.

Darran was given some very alarming news. His doctor told him that he had some kind of heart condition. This was to put the fear of god into him. Darran had a great love for life and had always looked after his body. He didn't smoke, didn't drink, but admitted to having a weakness for the ladies. Well, two out of three is not bad. He cried out to me:

"Why me Mum, why me?"

After a year of extensive tests at our local hospital as an outpatient, it was still not discovered what was wrong with him. He was put on medication but Darran's problem still stayed with him.

Eventually he was seen by a young up and coming specialist, who informed Darran he was on the wrong medication, and was to advise him that his problem was too high a level of adrenaline, and that there was nothing wrong with his heart at all. His medication was changed and Darran very quickly lost the unpleasant symptoms that he had suffered from for nearly two years. This medication it seems he will have to take for the rest of his life, but what a relief all round to know his heart was strong.

Although Darran doesn't like to party, he loves talking and listening to people who have something of interest to relate.

He loves his family very much, from the oldest to the youngest. He has a great sense of humour and can be very entertaining when he chooses to be.

He claims to suffer from a compulsive disorder, and also has a fear of flying but has made it quite clear to me that if I ever decide to fly to Australia to visit with Teddy, his older brother, he was to go with me. He would say, "If anything is going to happen to you Mum, It's going to happen to me too; I'm not ready to lose you yet".

After several unsuccessful relationships, Darran at last, in his early thirties, finally met the young woman who is definitely his soul mate. The fact that she has three children from her first marriage was in fact a bonus for Darran; he loves them to bits.

When Darran's daughter Holly was nine years old and having a lot of problems at home, he was approached by Holly's mum to be reunited with his daughter. We tried our very best, but Holly's problems were too deeply rooted. She was so full of resentment and was so unresponsive that after two years we gave up. All the time that Holly had the problems she had at home Darran and I didn't stand a chance. We were to try again for a second time because Holly was being so unruly, but with little success. I believe she is now living with a young man and is completely estranged from her Mother. If Holly ever wants to make contact in her adult life, if she can ever rid her mind of the unjust accusations that have been placed there by her mother, she would be welcomed with open arms. Speaking for myself, she is still my granddaughter and I still love her. The large picture of her that still hangs on my wall along with all the other grandchildren is a constant reminder of a sweet and innocent child of nine months old, that I had held in my arms more than eighteen years before.

Darran it seems has so far lived quite a complex life. I have sometimes wondered if in fact he carried a self-destruct button around with him, as he has had to cope with and overcome so many obstacles in his life. Maybe his excessive adrenaline problem, to some extent, is responsible. Darran is loving and loyal and appreciates his family ties. He visits me on Sundays and enjoys a roast dinner with his mum. He keeps in touch with his dad and has grown very fond of Debbie, his dad's second wife. My gratitude goes out to her for the way in which she accepted Darran and took him to heart.

When these kinds of situations are handled correctly, it can make such a difference to a young child growing up. I knew she was a nice person before I even met her. I always listened to Darran singing her praises whenever he was to return from a visit with them both.

Darran and Sara still live apart although they are convinced they are right for each other, they both feel they should break the children in gradually; I feel certain that they will do the job right.

Darran was sharing a flat with a female friend and whilst this had worked very well for them both (Nicky was indeed a lovely natured girl) it proved to be causing some unrest in his relationship with Sara. Darran asked my opinion and I told him it should not be difficult to understand Sara's attitude towards this situation, especially as Nicky was an ex girlfriend.

This relationship had not lasted long and was long over by the time that Darran and Sara had become an item. So it was that Darran moved into a flat of his own: his expenses jumped up, but his life was more, peaceful.

For company, Darran installed a fish tank and bought two black moor fish. Within days one of the fish died, so he replaced it with another black moor; the same thing happened again. The shop advised him to try a different fish. This Darran did on two more occasions, and still the fish died. The shop assistant suggested he had got himself a rogue fish. When I saw Darran the following Sunday, I asked him how was he getting on with his fish problem.

"I'm not beat yet Mum," he declared, "I think I've got a serial killer on my hands. It's even destroying the plants by actually head butting them!"
I believe Darran has now solved the problem. He has put some really tiny fish in with his serial killer, and because the little fish dart about so quickly, the black moor hasn't a fin to float on. He also increased the amount of food he is feeding them.

Darran has now inherited a grey talking parrot, which seems to give him a great deal of pleasure. Darran would dearly love to have a dog, but it wouldn't be fair to the animal as he works all day and on most evenings visits Sara and the children.

Although my story as far as Darran is concerned has come to a standstill, I firmly believe that Darran, because of Sara and the children: Richard, Grant and Anna-Marie, at the age of thirty-five, has only now found his true path in life.

I wish them both much happiness in the future. I feel happy in the knowledge that there is a very strong bond between them; strong enough to see them through the knocks that life itself seems always able to send their way. So I close this chapter by stating how much I love you Darran and how much I'm looking forward to next Sunday when we will once again have dinner together and either chat or watch a good film on the Telly.

Anytime I spend with my sons is a big part of my life force. If anything were to happen to any one of them, it would be like a light going out that would leave me floundering in a dark place.

Darran's daughter Holly

CHAPTER TWENTY-THREE

The Death of my Father

We had as a family all felt that Mum would be the one that we would lose first because of the weakness in her lungs.

Dad was so strong in body, mind and character, and hardly ever felt the need to see a doctor. He was always so full of life, and if he felt in really good spirits, you would quite often catch him dancing a little tap dance.

The day came that I received a phone call from Chrissy, the baby of the family, to say Dad hadn't turned up for his tea as had been arranged for that day. This had caused Chrissy to phone him, but she couldn't get an answer. So she had made her way to his house, again to receive no response.

"I'm going to break in," she cried. "I can hear the dog whining".

"Please wait for me Chris," I said, but she thought Dad could be in trouble and could need help.

So I put on my coat and dashed over to Dads; it took me less than five minutes to get there. Chrissy had broken a window, opened the door and let the dog out. The poor thing had been holding its water for about as long as it was possible.

Chrissy met me on the pathway and fell into my arms.

"O, Bett," she cried out, "Our dad is dead!"

Strange as it may seem, I could not cry at this point, but just held Chrissy in my arms until her tears slowly ceased. My brother Robert arrived, and then the doctor. The doctor's remarks were to stay with me always.

"What a young and good looking man your father is."

He could not believe Dad's age of seventy-five. It seemed as if in death all the stresses of life had fallen away from his face.

"You won't think so at this time, but you will later realize what a fortunate way this was for your father to go."
As a doctor he claimed he was called out at times to witness horrific deaths. But Dad was sitting on the settee, the telly still on, and he had nodded off for a little nap. I looked at him. There was a terrible tightness in my chest. He looked so cold and distant, but a little voice in my head told me it wasn't my Dad, it was only a shell; Dad has gone to wherever it is that our loved one's go.

I went home and sat on the bottom of the stairs just looking at the phone. I felt numb; still this terrible tightness in my chest, and still could not cry. I don't know how long I had been sitting there. My son Garry was the first person to arrive home.

Although he claimed he knew something was terribly wrong by the look on my face, he had no idea what. He put his arms around me, and that is when the tears came - my poor son just stood there until I was done. He was shocked to hear Dad was dead. He claimed he had appeared to be so fit and well.

Coronary Thrombosis, I believe is a clot of blood that blocks the main valve to the heart. The worse was yet to come. I had to find the courage to tell Mum. She was to quietly cry for days and days. It never fails to amaze me how resilient us humans can be when faced with the sort of aching pain that grief can bring us.

The date for Dad's funeral was set, and we went about clearing Dad's house. We would have liked to have left this job until after the funeral, but the council expected us to do the right thing, so they could get another family off their housing list as soon as possible. The boys dealt with the big stuff, furniture and the like, and us girls packed clothes, books and handed out mementoes to family members.

We placed a blanket on the floor in the middle of the room and began taking Dad's books out of the bookcase and putting them onto the blanket with the intention of taking them to his village charity shop. I stopped and retrieved a book as something had caught my eye.

"Look at this girls," I declared, and waved a twenty-pound note under their noses.

"Well," Chrissy said, "This means we've got to go through all these books one by one."

And there were quite a number of them.

At the end of our search we collected together almost £1,000. Although Dad had a bank account, he always liked to have money handy. He still used to do a little wheeling and dealing in his retirement. Old habits, it seems, die hard.

In Dad's personal papers I found a postcard that he had sent to me wishing me a happy 10th birthday whilst he was serving in the Royal Marine's during the war. This find was to give me great comfort; to think he had hung onto it all these years.

Dad had always told us not to wear black at his funeral, but we found we couldn't do this. However we all wore coloured scarves to ease our conscience. Dad was buried at Church In The Wood, Hollington. The church itself was full of family members and there was a crowd of people outside; some I knew, but others were strangers to me. Who were all these people? They all looked so sad and solemn. I went around after the service and shook hands with all of them; they obviously knew Dad well.

Mum never made the graveside. Her legs gave way. She was supported by two members of the family - one each side of her and they stood in hearing distance a few feet away. The Marine Soldier who stood in the church beside Dad's coffin had to report back to duty, so was taken to the railway station and sent off with our thanks ringing in his ears. He was a most charming young man. We were sad to see him go, it was almost as if he was part of our Dad. But of course, we knew it was probably the Royal Marine uniform, nevertheless his presence at our Dad's funeral meant so much to us.

Some months later, I had a persistent urge to travel to Cranbrooke in Kent, which was where my father had been born and spent most of his youth. He had spoken to me of his regular pub that he had spent many hours socializing in, and I remembered him pointing it out to me once or twice when we were travelling through Cranbrooke on our way to the hop gardens. I found myself wondering whether I would be able to find it. So, I set off. On arriving in Cranbrooke I parked my car and began to walk, allowing my memory to guide me.

Cranbrooke is not a very large place so there was not much ground for me to cover. I found it in no time at all, a small pub situated in the main shopping area. I stepped inside, ordered a half pint of shandy and sat myself down at a corner table that allowed me to view the whole area, especially the bar. I sat quietly sipping my drink and listening to the chatter of the half a dozen people enjoying a lunchtime beer. I was imagining my Dad there with them, but as a young man. It proved to be the most extraordinary experience for me. I allowed my mind to travel back in time, remembering the stories that Dad had relayed to all of us. I suddenly became totally unaware of the people there. I could feel my father all around me; tears were forming in my eyes. I wasn't handling these strange sensations very well at all. I almost ran out of the pub. My dad had filled me and it was a few moments before I could breathe calmly.

It was a very moving experience, but also rather strange. I believe it was too soon for me to have made that visit, and I must admit I have not tried to repeat going there again. Not for any reason other than the fact that the level of emotion was just too much for me to contain.

CHAPTER TWENTY-FOUR

Letting Mum Go

Mum was in hospital receiving treatment following a really bad bronchial attack. On her last day before being allowed back home, she was to confide in me that the stairs at home were becoming very difficult for her and that Mary, my sister, had suggested that Mum should go to her because Mary had a large house with two sitting rooms, plus a downstairs room that could be used as a bedroom. Also, Mother declared, that I myself had really earned a good rest.

Mary and her husband Eric only lived a ten-minute walk away and I would be able to visit Mum frequently. I also believe that Mum had realised to some extent that her coming to me in the first instance had in fact hurt Mary's feelings. So these new arrangements would please Mary, and give her the chance to do her bit for our Mum. Mary had wanted to be the one to approach me on this delicate subject, but it was Mum who pleaded with Mary that it should in fact be her.

As time went on Mum became more and more housebound, and when it was suggested that we buy for her a wheelchair, it did not go down very well at all. With a promise to buy her a really nice one, her six children between them collected enough money to do just that. But Mum was obviously finding the idea of being wheeled around in a wheelchair an embarrassing prospect.

Every year, in the month of September, we would make a nostalgic visit to the hop gardens. These visits would always leave us feeling quite emotional. Mother would often drop a tear and say that it was at these hop-picking times that she would have the family all together, in close proximity for at least six weeks. It was hard work, but she loved every minute of it. So it was on one of these visits that brother Jim along with Mary, Chrissy, and myself planned a picnic as a surprise for Mum. Sadly, she was now in her wheelchair, but

Jim's strong arms seemed to make the task of dragging the wheelchair along the muddy furrows easy going. All of us were laughing as Mum was being bumped along at a steady pace. Suddenly, one of the wheels hit a mound of hard earth, and the chair turned onto its side and gently, almost in slow motion tipped Mother out. Jim secured her back into the chair and we all sat down and gathered around her. We all burst out with uncontrollable laughter that seemed to go on for ages. Mary was the first to collect herself together.

"Right," she said, "we'll have the picnic here shall we?"

So we did. It proved to be a really enjoyable and delightful afternoon.

Some weeks later, Mary and I told her we would take her and the chair by car to the nearest shopping town other than Hastings (our hometown), that being Eastbourne. We decided to drive straight into the car park of a major shopping precinct. Mum was beginning to enjoy being able to visit so many shops. She had not had this pleasure for some considerable time. There was just one slight problem. You would not believe the number of people from Hastings that stopped to talk to us and say how lovely it was to see Mum out and about again. Mum took us both to task by stating:

"So much for the promise you two made that nobody would know us over here in Eastbourne".

We all ended up with a good giggle and a visit to a café for a nice cup of tea and toasted teacake. As for the wheelchair, it was put to constant use. It was one thing taking care of Mum, but there was always the constant stream of family visitors to make tea for. Fourteen grandchildren and four great grandchildren were to follow, not forgetting of course her own six children and their partners. You sometimes felt you were running a railway buffet. To Mum, her family was her life, and the more housebound she became, the more she would look out for her visitors. She was relying more and more on her tot of whiskey that she would have in her tea twice a day. The doctor was making more and more regular visits.

Mary was beginning to look very drained, as Mother became ever more demanding. I think Mum knew her time was near; she would now be waking Mary up quite regularly during the night and wanting Mary to sit in the bedroom with her until she fell asleep. I now believe that Mum was afraid of the coming of death.

Chrissy and I talked, and agreed that Mum needed night and day care. We also realized that Mary would not agree to Mum being placed in a nursing home, but this time Mary was looking so totally exhausted, so she gave Chrissy and I little opposition. We made sure that Mary realised that this decision was ours, not hers.

So with all her six children paying what they could afford, Mum was placed in a nursing home that was situated nearby. A really lovely place named 'Ledsham Court', situated on the Ridge, Hastings. All the family made regular visits. Chrissy and I went to see and sit with her every day. Mary was to visit Mum twice every day. We made sure that Mum had her constant supply of whiskey, and the matron was quite happy to let us do so. ·

Mum was there only a few months when her time came to leave us. We three girls were with her, and sat softly talking to her, and although she couldn't talk to us I knew she could hear us. I told her that all the family were present, but in fact most arrived too late to see Mum alive. It had been difficult to track them all down; so many were not at home, some were at work, some shopping, but eventually most were able to be contacted and they arrived in a steady stream. So much grief, so many tears, but then that is the ultimate price that must be paid when you lose a loving mother and grandmother.

Mum came from country stock and loved the wild flowers. Her favourite was the bright yellow primrose and was the favourite of her own mother before her. On another occasion the previous year, we girls had taken Mum and the wheelchair, plus a picnic to the hop gardens just prior to them being harvested. There was no one about so we slipped in through the gate and dragged the wheelchair with Mum in it along a furrow between the hop bines and spent an hour enjoying our picnic and taking in the smell and atmosphere of the hops. This has proved to be a very memorable time for us girls and Mum did so enjoy her trip down memory lane that day.

Our Chrissy felt she hadn't grieved for Mum, as she should have done, because she was still grieving for the loss of her husband Chris, who died just five weeks before Mum.

Darran, bless him was soothed by the fact that his nan had managed to see his birthday, the 3rd of May, which was the day before she had died.

It's very sad that there are some grandchildren and great grandchildren who were never able to enjoy or really know this wonderful and loving woman. Fortunately memory allows me to reflect and relate precious moments from my past and for this I will be eternally grateful.

Mum was buried with Dad at the cemetery of 'Church in the Wood', Hollington, and may they forever rest in peace.

Love never dies if you choose to nurture it; and I have chosen.

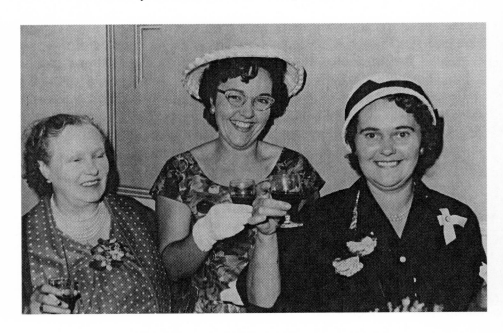

Mum's Sister Flo, niece Mary and my Mum

CHAPTER TWENTY-FIVE

Family Unity

Is it money, music, or love that makes the world go around? Well, in all honesty, it is, I believe, all three.

Make no mistake about it, any existence without these things in life that most of us take for granted, is a desolate existence to say the least.

In war people come together and become strong in their unity, because they are threatened, they automatically seek strength from each other. In times of peace it seems we are very self-indulgent. But there are those that strive the whole of their lives to contribute to the quality of life for all. These types of people who exist amongst us are very necessary to keep some sort of acceptable balance in our day-to-day existence. My sister Mary is one of these; she delights in giving pleasure and help to those that need it. Sometimes referred to as do-gooders, but these people do serve as a balance to the order of things, when you consider the more decadent and the like that live amongst us, and that they come from all walks of life - all the more reason to believe in family unity and the importance of family life.

As a child, Mother would say I could talk the hind legs off a donkey, and nick named me 'chatterbox'. Father would often threaten to stick an apple in my mouth and would declare that if I had been born an Indian (Native American), I would have been named 'Cave in the Face'. Having said that, he would then hug me and tell me how beautiful I was. This bit of fun had no lasting ill effect on me because I knew Dad was just funning. I also knew that many family members would be standing with a hand on their forehead after just ten minutes listening to my endless chatter. As I got older, still with this awareness in the back of my mind, try as I would, I could not control this endless onslaught. But I was truly loved none the less, and tolerated with a patience that can be termed (as father would put it) as trying the patience of Jobe himself.

My brothers and sisters all were given double Christian names, whereas I was only given one, 'Rebecca'. Maybe they thought that the name said it all. Unlike many of my schoolmates, I did indeed like the name my parents had bestowed upon me. As I grew older I began to realize that I should have taken down notes from older family members, because once they were gone, so much information was forever lost.

Ted's half brother Richard phoned me recently, and at the age of about sixty he became painfully aware that he did not have a photograph of any kind of his mother Helen. I searched all through my photo albums and, I could not believe I did not have one. I proceeded to phone around the family in hopes that someone would have a photo that I could pass onto him. So far I have had no luck at all. Helen died whilst I was in the very early stages of my marriage to her son Ted, and neither Ted nor myself had the joy of owning a camera.

In the years between 1950-1960 it was not unusual for families to be without a family camera, unlike today, 2004; it would be quite unusual to find a family without one. My heart goes out to Richard and his family. Whilst I have only a few photos of my Mum and Dad, I haven't any of them when they were young, but at least I have some photographs to pass on down the family line.

Although I'm almost completely wrapped up in my family, I do have many acquaintances, too many to mention in fact, but there are a few people outside the boundaries of my direct family that I care about a great deal.

My first cousin Violet is a darling and she is just a few years older than me and is a beautiful woman, even at the age of eighty-two she still has that twinkle in her eyes that I have always associated with her and her personality. When I was in my early teens, I had a terrible crush on Derek, her husband, a lovely man who sadly died in his early forties.

A friend of twenty years is a man named Tony Hughes. He is strong in character and has proved to be honest and loyal - three characteristics that I admire in a person.

There is Val and her partner Paul. Val has been my dancing partner for many a Saturday night out for over twenty-five years. Paul patiently sits and enjoys the live music while sipping his beer. He's just happy to see us enjoying our dancing.

What is love? I could say its butterflies in the stomach. I could say it's a weakness in the knees. But life itself has taught me that it's as simple as realising that you love someone more than you love yourself, whoever that person may be.

Grief is something that walks hand in hand with love all our lives. The balance between these two elements can vary from one person to another. As a child we grieve being taken away from the breast, or bottle, sometimes the good old standby, the dummy, or 'soother' as some call it. We grieve when being wrenched away from a Mother's arms to attend school. We grieve the loss of a girlfriend or boyfriend, or when having to face the death of a loving father or mother. We grieve far more than any of us realise, but as a species we are so very resilient. To be loved is a very necessary pleasure - a natural healer to enhance our well being and encourage healthy growth.

Sex is the driving force of nature that few of us can claim to be indifferent to. At the age of seventy I believe I have long reached a point in time where I can safely say that food can reach parts of me that man cannot. Sex for me now, is likely to be a good lean steak (medium rare), fried onions, tomatoes, mushrooms and a good portion of fried chips. Not very wise, but then, in this day and age, neither is sex.

Loyalty and honesty should be part of family life. If you have a loving caring family you are rich indeed. Not everyone is so blessed.

CHAPTER TWENTY-SIX

Hastings & History

Hastings is steeped in History. My mind is searching its memory banks in case I have forgotten anything that might be of interest and importance to my family in the future.

I know one thing: if somebody was to hand me a book that was dated back in time, of my family history, I would be enthralled - but the likelihood of that is zero. So my feelings at this moment in time are very satisfying and I have a sense of achievement. My thanks goes to Margaret Thatcher who made it possible for me to buy my council house from Hastings Council; she is at present celebrating twenty five years service to the Conservative Party, 1979-2004. When she became the very first woman to become Prime Minister of England, she was given the nickname, 'The Iron Lady'.

I have memories of the Prince Albert Memorial Clock that stood in the centre of Hastings main shopping area. It was vandalised in 1972 and taken down, with some parts being placed in storage. There was a huge outcry, but it was to no avail. People still today when travelling on the bus will ask for the memorial stop, even though it is no longer there.

Our local cricket ground where Ted and I had taken the boys to watch a game of cricket, and where we would sit on the grass and enjoy a sunny afternoon picnic, has since been levelled out and a shopping precinct built on the site, called 'Priory Meadow'.

On the Hastings shoreline, a ship that lies almost completely buried in sand, and can only be seen at very low tide should be treasured. It has been dated 1749 and history tells us that mutiny aboard was the cause of its unfortunate fate. It was decided at some point that to retrieve it would be far too costly. There is a strong possibility that we will lose it altogether if plans go ahead to reinforce the coastline. The name of the ship was 'The Amsterdam'.

Many times our shores have been invaded. The best well known is the 'Battle of Hastings' that took place in 1066, and was actually fought outside of Hastings at a place called Battle. King Harold II had already encountered heavy fighting in the North of England against his evil brother Tostig who had teamed up with the King of Norway, Harald Hardrada. Both were slain in a devastating battle at Stamford Bridge. Harold's victory was to finally free Britain from Scandinavia.

At the beginning of October news reached Harold of a second invasion in the South by Duke William who believed that Harold's crown should have been his and he was prepared to fight for it. Harold arrived seven miles north of Hastings with his tired and tattered army hoping to surprise the Normans. But William was ready and on the 14th October 1066 a bloody battled was to eventually bring about the death of Harold. Killed it is written by an arrow in the right eye. The battle was fought over quite a large area: Telham Hill, Battle Hill and Senlac Hill.

It is thought that Harold was buried on the seashore on William's orders. A monastery was built, Battle Abbey, and it still stands today alongside the town of Battle. William was crowned King on Christmas Day 1066.

A part of folk law history is a giant of a man called 'Jack in the Green', who we celebrate every year on Mayday. He's dressed totally in a green leafy suit and wearing a leafy crown. He is pursued by many dancing and frolicking followers who eventually catch him and bring him down to the ground and slay him. This act is professed to release the 'Spirit of Summer'. To me, it calls out of witches, witches caverns and cauldrons. He always seems to be accompanied by the Morris Dancers who I feel use the language of dance to express life, and again the Spirit of Summer. The Spirit of Summer is released on the 1st of May. On the first Sunday in the month of May, we experience the daunting sight of hundreds of bikers descending on Hastings. What this is all about, I really have no idea. They are a good crowd and are well behaved. The locals get a chance to see some really impressive machines.

Hastings Pier, built in 1872, has in recent years undergone repairs and refurbishment and was re-opened to the public in 2002. Unfortunately, the St Leonards Palace Pier, although built at a later date and officially opened to the public in 1891 at the overall cost of £30,000, was subjected to several accounts of bad luck and misfortune. It suffered severe damage from a bomb attack in 1940, followed by more damage by fire. It was never re-opened to the public. In March 1951, after damage by a severe gale, the Hastings Corporation completed the demolition of the Pier. Apparently it had been a most elegant structure with gold and maroon furnishings. It comprised of two refreshment rooms, and the finest saloon lounge to be found in the borough. Concerts, opera, ballet and plays were performed almost all year round. Dances to popular bands were held twice weekly. It held Bluebird summertime concert parties, roller-skating, and an American bowling alley, and also boasted exceptional angling facilities.

There are two exciting tourist attractions to visit. The 1066 Story in Hastings Castle and the Smugglers Adventure in St Clements Caves have plenty of history and literature at a reasonable price. The opening of the West Hill lift to the public was in March 1891. The County Borough of Hastings subsequently purchased it in April 1947. Two passenger cars work in opposite directions, up a gradient of 1 in 3. The original drive was by means of a gas engine, replaced at some point in time by a diesel oil engine. In 1971 it was replaced yet again, only this time with an electric motor. Passengers on reaching the top of the hill are treated to a stunning view of Hastings Old Town and the fisherman's beach. The East Hill lift came a little later. It was completed in the spring of 1902. The opening took place on April 9th 1902, the Coronation Day of Edward VII. He reigned from 1901-1910. It was a water balanced passenger lift. The water tanks were built into the top station. The cars each had a 600-gallon water tank. Sadly the water balance system was replaced with an electric motor and cost somewhere in the region of £35,000. I believe this work took place in 1974. Down through the years the East Hill lift has soaked up much more money than was ever intended. During World War II, the army commanded the lift in order to supply the military installation on the East Hill.

Last, but by no means least, is our beautiful 'Alexandra Park'. Originally laid out by Robert Marnock, a Landscape Gardener, in 1878 and opened by the Prince and Princess of Wales on June 26th 1882. It consists of 109 acres. The park is registered in the 'Register of Parks & Gardens of Special Historic Interest', and boasts many rare trees, one of which is the 'Champion Tree'. The park is now undergoing extensive restoration work in the years of 2000-2004, and is supported by the National Lottery through the Heritage Lottery Fund.

In the year 2000, I participated in the celebrations of the Millennium, 1,000 Years of History. Not everyone will live through and experience the like in their lifetime.

At this time of writing, the year 2004, it seems that our shores are being invaded yet again. Only this time it seems the culprits are illegal immigrants. They bypass the system set up by the government that select suitable applicants who want to start a new life in this country. There is much unrest by the ordinary men and women in the street concerning the number of illegal immigrants managing to disappear into the system, and draining the country's resources such as the NHS and Social Security payouts. The government is talking about introducing Identity Cards for which we will pay approximately £35 - but surely do we not already have various forms of identification, such as driving license, bankcards, library cards and the rest. What is really needed in my opinion is for the law to make it possible for police to be able to approach anyone they suspect to be an illegal citizen without fear of accusation. This would be a positive start towards controlling the illegal immigrant problem and sorting it out.

History is constantly in the making; please let us make it right.

CHAPTER TWENTY-SEVEN

Memories

Because of that wonderful invention, the television, I have travelled the world far and wide and even to its furthest regions without leaving the safety of my own four walls.

Some people might view this information as rather sad, but I assure you it is not. I am an extremely bad traveller and suffer most unpleasant symptoms. I'm also allergic to medication that could help to alleviate this unpleasantness. The only form of travel that does not upset me is when I drive myself, in my car. I have seen and visited many parts of this island of ours and if I was to suffer anything at all, it would be an aching bum after driving over a certain amount of hours at a time. So you will understand how much I appreciate the fact that I can drive, and own a car. My grandchildren pass secret smiles when they find me talking to my car, and I must admit to playing it up because it gives them pleasure.

I often smile about the time I took Mum for a drive out into the country. I drove around all the country lanes and through small picturesque villages. We stopped at a small country pub and enjoyed a glass of shandy and something to eat. Then once again, back in the car we set off. It was such a lovely day and Mum was in good spirits; not being able to walk very much these days she did so love these outings in the car – however mum and I both have a poor sense of direction. She would sit with her hands resting in her lap and drink in all the sights, no idea at all where we were or where we were going, totally trusting my expertise at driving. Suddenly she looked at me and asked, "Why are you smiling to yourself my love?"

"Mum," I said, "for the last half hour I've been trying not to panic, but I have to tell you that we are lost."
I had no idea where I was or which turning to take that would point me in the direction of home.

"We can't keep driving around," said Mum. "Whatever will you do?"

"Don't worry Mum, I'll keep driving around until I come across a place I know."

My dear Mother, ever trusting, continued to drink in the wonderful view that a sunny summer's day gives to us all, and of course, finally we ended up back home safe and sound.

Some years back Ted and I bought a second-hand Ford Fiesta that was only two years old. The Ford Fiesta first appeared in 1977. It was our pride and joy. We started off with an old banger and worked our way up over a number of years to this final purchase. I was driving home one day when I noticed in my rear view mirror a police car directly behind me. Nothing unusual in that but I was becoming concerned when on the final approach to my home they were still close behind me. I pulled to a stop, and got out of the car; they did likewise. I breathed a sigh of relief when they approached me with such pleasant smiles on their faces, indicating to me that nothing was seriously wrong. All sorts of things flash through your mind when being approached by the Police. I asked if I had done something wrong; if in some way my driving had been at fault.

"On the contrary," they both said, "your driving was in fact excellent." I looked at them a little puzzled. "Unfortunately you are driving a stolen vehicle!" They proceeded to ask me to hand over the keys, which of course I did. Big mistake; possession was still nine tenths of the law. There was no need for a lawyer to prove that we had purchased in good faith. We never saw the car again, or our money. That left us to start all over again, and this we did. Ted had been very kind and understanding about me handing over the keys. But if my memory serves me right, when I first gave him the news, his first reaction was to call me a silly cow, and of course he was right.

There was another occasion when I felt a little silly. I began receiving letters; they arrived by post at monthly intervals. Whilst they were not threatening in themselves, I began to feel intimidated, so I took them to the police who decided they were no real threat, and as I didn't have any idea who the culprit was, there was not much they could do about it. As time went on the letters became more personal and very suggestive and still they were delivered one letter a month as was usual. Darran decided he would take them to the police, and this time after reading them the police decided they had changed their minds and would now be very interested. We were to give to them any information we could and report anything unusual.

When the next monthly letter arrived, and still no sign that the police were going to resolve anything, Darran asked me to give him all the letters. He spread them all out and read them very carefully, and he began to piece together bits of written information; like putting a puzzle together.

"Mother" he declared, "I think I've got him."
In one of the letters, his father's two cars were mentioned. In another, a river that flowed at the back of his house was mentioned where nude young girls would swim. He would often state where he was going, and other letters would mention landmarks. The latest letter mentioned his 10 o'clock dental appointment. Darran was also able to piece together roughly the area where the man lived.

"I've checked it out Mum," he said, "there is only one dentist in that area; I'll sit in my car and wait to see who turns up for a 10 o'clock appointment."

This Darran did. On the day stated at 10 o'clock a man arrives at the dentist; slim build, long mousy hair, and baggy clothes with cut down Wellington boots. Darran followed him at a reasonable distance. The car stopped outside a house in Rye and the man disappeared inside. Darran noticed straight away the two cars in the driveway matching the description in one of the letters. He then drives his car around to the back of this house and sure enough, there was the small river that had also been described. Darran, having promised me faithfully that he would not intercept this person himself, took the information straight to the police. The police congratulated Darran on his detective work, and did indeed act on the information. I was assured that the matter had been dealt with, and that I should not receive any more letters. I found myself relaxing a little; I had spent months just constantly looking over my shoulder. When the next monthly letter arrived, I couldn't believe it. Who would defy the police in this way, especially as they knew their address was no secret. Darran studied the letter, then again took it to the police. They told Darran they had spoken to an elderly gentleman.

"The man I followed was about thirty years old," stated Darran. With the police assuring him that they would make another trip out to Rye, Darran came home.

"Mother," he said, "If the police don't resolve this problem, I will."

To my relief the letters stopped. The police must have driven home their message on their second trip with much more authority. Apparently this man had a previous record for exactly the same offence.

I was terrified of Darran getting into trouble with the law himself. He had controlled his anger so well and I'm not sure if I could have deterred him from his instinctive need to protect his Mum.

I certainly didn't know this person. Did he just pick me out of the phone book, or did he see me shopping in Ore Village and follow me home? My anxieties over this matter were to stay with me for some considerable time. I believe for me it was the fact that I didn't know what sort of person he was, and to what extent he was likely to go. A small part of me was asking, was there something that I had done to attract this sort of person to me? I know that there are many worse cases, but believe me, being stalked by letter is bad enough.

Down through the years, I have discovered that I am allergic to many substances; none thankfully that could be fatal to me, but could cause for me unpleasant symptoms. With knowledge and experience, I've been able to avoid coming in contact with most of these substances and obtain a quality of happy well being. It's very likely that along with my strong genes, I will undoubtedly pass on some if not all of these allergies of mine, for which I am truly sorry.

During my married life of twenty-five years, there was not the time or even the energy for either myself or Ted to indulge ourselves, and money was always sparse. So it seems after our divorce, and whilst I was in my late forties, I found myself taking up modelling for Eastex, swanning around the dining tables at Plummers Restaurant and the Queens Hotel that was situated on Hastings seafront. I did this for a few years and enjoyed this work very much. I also started writing poetry. This seemed to come to me very easily, and a sense of satisfaction would stay with me.

Grandchildren are well and truly on the scene now and are the delight of my life, but more about them later.

At the age of sixty-six, it was time for me to sell the house at Churchill Avenue. I'd lived there for forty-five years, but it was now too much for me to want to cope with. At the time it was a very emotional wrench for me, even the grandchildren made their feelings felt; they did not want to leave the house. I explained that we would only be leaving bricks and mortar, and would be taking all our love and memories with us to wherever nanny would be living. This seemed to appease them. The people who bought my house sent me a lovely letter thanking me for the way I had cleaned the place - I had left them a note saying I'd left curtains up so they could all collapse into bed after a long and tiring day moving. I'd left odd plates and mugs, sugar, milk and teabags and some cutlery. They had two very young children and where grateful to me for my thoughtfulness. But I was also saying thank you and goodbye to my home, silly me! My sons were brilliant, they made it so easy for me - they arranged everything.

I had put my name forward for a two bedroom flat in a brand new building housing one hundred and twenty five flats, and over looking our beautiful park. It took me almost a year before I could call it home. In the first few months, my car would take me several times up the hill that led to Churchill Avenue, and I would have to turn the car around and point it in the direction of my flat.

Me on the catwalk

Alexandra Park Mansions is designed to accommodate people over fifty-five. Quite a few people here still go out to work - these are the people who usually lose out on a parking space. Others have long realized that if they are home before three o'clock, their car will be accommodated with a space!

I have a smile and pleasant attitude for everyone - but of course there are problems, humans being what they are, a complex mixture of all types. You'd be a very clever person indeed if you were able to please everyone. I frown on any form of gossip. I suppose it's true to say I don't mix in all that well, and choose not to join in with all the social activity available here. I have a full family life, but I also enjoy the comfort and relaxation that my home provides for me.

If I had moved here in my fifties as opposed to later on in my sixties, I may well have at times joined in on the festivities. To put my feet up and enjoy a daily glass of my favourite sherry, and watch a film or listen to some good music suits me just fine. Oh, by the way, my nickname here, as I've been told, is 'Lady Becky'.

It was about this time, having so much more time to myself that I began to write poetry in earnest. My son Garry has his own recording facilities at his home, and offered to record me reading my poems and place them on a CD - I was thrilled! He also recorded me singing some of the very old songs that my grand Mother had sung to my Dad, and who in turn had sung them to me.

"This way," Garry said, "they won't be forgotten."

Garry was once a guest on BBC Radio Three, and he took my CD of old songs with him. The programme was called 'Music Matters', and being discussed was music from the Romany Travellers life. Disappointingly, it was not actually played, so my CD is tucked away somewhere in the BBC archives. Whether they will ever use it or not is something else.

I've mentioned very little of Romany life; in truth I don't feel inclined to write too much about a subject that I have not experienced for myself, as in living out there on the road travelling freely. In spirit, I feel life and living very deeply within myself, and I have strong family ties, and I am very proud of my Mum and Dad and the strong values that they passed down to me and mine. Much of what was passed down to me stemmed from Romany teachings; love, family unity and cleanliness has walked hand in hand with me from as far back as I can remember.

My grandchildren; I refer to them as being a gift of love. They are growing up so very fast and whilst they each as individuals do have their occasional problems, they are very well adjusted to everyday life, and will go on to lead a full and hopefully happy existence.

Tom, at the age of seventeen and still at school, works weekends to boost his spending money. He is very artistic and although he has no idea or plans for his future as yet, he is a very intelligent young man and I'm certain he will do well whatever path he decides to take.
I personally have felt for three years now that he will become a writer at some time in his life.
Eddy, his young brother at the age of fifteen has the ability to be anything he sets his mind to. He has a very high IQ and like his father, Garry, has a natural ability regarding music. Eddy has already formed a young band and successfully realised his first gig for a private party. Talk about history repeating itself! Tanya, my granddaughter, works for Virgin Airlines and keeps in touch. Tony, her brother, now in his twenties, lives a full and busy lifestyle. Sadly I see very little of him these days. Holly, of course I don't see at all. Maybe one day she will knock on my door.

I have always found great joy in the time spent with my grand children, and I'm always ready with sound advice, but most importantly always found the time to sit and listen to them. Young people are under more pressure these days than ever before in the past.
Unfortunately, I never had the pleasure of grandparents - probably because my Mum, being the youngest of twenty-two children in all, found herself with parents who were getting on in years. I was three years old and both Mothers' parents were dead. Grandfather Henry Ripley died on 17th September 1934; he was seventy years old. Grandmother Priscilla Ripley, maiden name Beaney, died on the 9th

March 1937 aged sixty-seven years. They are buried together at Church in the Wood, Hastings. Their stone also pays tribute to their son Joseph Ripley who was killed in action on the 4th of November 1916 aged just twenty one.

My father's parents split up when he was very young. Sadly, I have no knowledge of grandfather Walter Bilsby, but Dad was able to pass on to me a photograph of his mother, Matilda Bilsby, maiden name Brazill. On the 11th November 1918 she was presented with a Kings message expressing greetings and gratitude for her efforts during World War I – signed King George R.I. On her deathbed it was first thought she was asking for water, but in fact she was asking for Walter. Although separated from him for a number of years, she must have continued to love him for the duration of her life.

My great grandparents were William and Maria Brazill. It is believed that great grandmother was Spanish, but it is uncertain where great grandfather originated. Maria died on 22nd April 1922 aged sixty-seven. William followed her on 13th April 1934 aged eighty-three. At Church in the Wood Cemetery, Hastings, you will find a great stone angel that measures from base to the tips of its wings an impressive nine feet. The epitaph reads:

> 'Gone is the face we loved so well
> Silent the voice we loved to hear
> Ti's sad but true, I wonder why
> The best are always the first to die
> Her loving ways and smiling face
> Are a pleasure to recall
> She had a kindly word for each
> And died beloved by all.'

Garry's children, Thomas and Eddy

Teddy's children, Tanya and Tony

My Mother's parents, Henry and Priscilla Ripley

The King's Message to the Royal Air Force.

To the Right Hon. Lord Weir, Secretary of State and President of the Air Council.

I N this supreme hour of victory I send greetings and heartfelt congratulations to all ranks of the Royal Air Force. Our aircraft have been ever in the forefront of the battle; pilots and observers have consistently maintained the offensive throughout the ever-changing fortunes of the day, and in the war zones our gallant dead have lain always beyond the enemies' lines or far out to sea.

OUR far-flung squadrons have flown over home waters and foreign seas, the Western and Italian battle lines, Rhineland, the mountains of Macedonia, Gallipoli, Palestine, the plains of Mesopotamia, the forests and swamps of East Africa, the North-West frontier of India, and the deserts of Arabia, Sinai, and Darfur.

THE birth of the Royal Air Force, with its wonderful expansion and development, will ever remain one of the most remarkable achievements of the Great War.

EVERYWHERE, by God's help, officers, men and women of the Royal Air Force have splendidly maintained our just cause, and the value of their assistance to the Navy, the Army, and to Home Defence has been incalculable. For all their magnificent work, self-sacrifice, and devotion to duty, I ask you on behalf of the Empire to thank them.

November 11th, 1918

George R. I.

To, M. Bilsby 16628 W.R.A.F.

The King's message to my grandmother, Matilda Bilsby

My great grandmother, Maria Brazil, wife of William Brazil

I'm aware that I am in the winter of my life cycle, but I refuse to allow myself to dwell too deeply on this fact. I feel pretty good in myself, and apart from having to take medication for blood pressure, and suffering the odd twinge here and there to my body, I'm pretty fit. I take my daily regular walk and never miss my daily intake of vitamin and mineral supplements, and although I enjoy my cup of tea and my daily glass of sherry, I make sure that I drink at least three pints of water a day. I made a visit to my doctor recently for my usual check up, and as I was leaving he proclaimed that whatever it was I was doing, I was to carry on doing it. He was obviously pleased with my present state of health, so therefore why shouldn't I be? I do in fact feel very fortunate. I see others my age, seventy and even younger, walking with the aid of a stick. I feel compassion for them, and I dread the idea - the possibility of not being able to take my daily walks. I do enjoy getting out and about. Summertime walks of course are favourable. Living opposite such a beautiful park - to see such an abundance of colourful flowerbeds, various types of great wonderful trees and the green, green of the grass. To watch young children running and laughing while playing. Sometimes there are tears if they should fall, but they soon recover. Sunday afternoons you can sit in a deck chair and listen to a local brass band. There is an impressive bandstand that provides the musicians with plenty of shade, or even shelter from a summer shower. A park café close by supplies food, drinks various, and of course the ever summertime delight, an ice cream. There is fierce competition from a nearby ice-cream van that sells the soft ice-cream variety, which I must admit is my favourite. Sometimes on a Sunday I will pop down to this van with a container and ask for two pounds worth (in money of course) of ice cream, bring it back to my flat and pop it in the freezer and serve it up after the Sunday lunch with whatever I have in mind for sweet. Sometimes while the Sunday joint is slowly cooking (I do love the meat to be tender), I will take a second walk around the park. I'm not one for sitting on park benches often because I just love to walk, but on occasion I do, and when I do, I lean back, close my eyes and lift my face to the sky and let the sun in its now weaker state, seep into me and soothe my senses. This experience leaves me with such a sense of contentment and relaxation - a feeling of just being at one with myself. It makes me very aware of what I will, at some point in time have to leave behind. What a gift life is. I content myself with the fact that I will live on in my children and in my grandchildren. It never fails to amaze me how much peace of mind this fact in itself gives to me, and once again instils in me the faith I have in family awareness. So many allow their families to drift apart. I do realise the very strong need to create one's own destiny, but surely it would not be too difficult to keep in touch.

Would I want to live my life all over again? The answer is yes I would, and with all that I've learnt and experienced I would be able to pass on to my loved ones. I remember my Dad saying if he could put his head on my shoulders what a fantastic start to life he would be able to give to me. But of course that kind of statement belongs somewhere like 'Never Never Land' and my Dad was no Peter Pan - bit of a Walter Mitty maybe, but no Peter Pan. Very strict and loving - he was the iron hand in a velvet glove.

CHAPTER TWENTY-EIGHT

My 70ᵗʰ Surprise Party

Just prior to my 70th birthday my sisters, Mary and Chrissy approached me and asked would I like a family party.

"Oh no," I replied, "don't do that. That's too expensive and too time consuming for you both."
I suggested that they take me out for a quiet birthday meal and this they both reluctantly agreed to do.

"Okay," they said in unison, "if that's what you want, then that's what we will do."

Well, this scheming conniving pair kept me completely in the dark; they both knew they would have to be very shrewd because they knew very well - I would not be easily fooled. They drew on the help of my niece Tracey and commenced to plan this family get together for my 70th.

Two days before my birthday they both instructed me to dress really well because they were taking me to a very posh place for this special meal. They had planned this event for the Saturday evening nearest my birthday.

On the evening of my 70th, my two sons, Garry and Darran, along with their lovely ladies took me out to dinner. I was unaware at the time that they had already paid out towards the coming surprise party. So in fact they paid out twice. I was to feel a little guilty about this at a later date. My sisters had insisted it be a surprise party, so the boys had little choice but to put hands in pockets a second time. They were both very good natured about it.

Saturday evening and my sisters both arrived at 7.30pm sharp to whisk me off, but not until they had given me the once over and declared, "you'll do."

Chrissy said, "the meal is not until 8.30pm so we've got plenty of time to pop in and have a drink with your son Garry."

She claimed he was booked to play at a local club nearby to the hotel where we were to have this wonderful meal. I was delighted, and claimed that Garry had not mentioned that he was playing local that night.

"Probably because he knew you would be with us," declared Mary.

I really fell for all this hook and line, they were both reeling me in inch by inch.

Chrissy opened the club door and in we went. The place was packed full of people, the disc jockey was playing 'Congratulations', and slowly this sea of faces began, one in turn, to make themselves known to me. I dropped my handbag, put my hands to my face and desperately looked for something to hang on to. My knees went all wobbly; and everyone but anyone who was important to me was there. I was to enjoy a night to remember. What more could anyone wish for but family and friends to share this time, with a table that boasted a beautiful display of flowers, a birthday cake and various foods to tempt the taste buds.

I did the rounds and lost count of how many hugs and kisses were exchanged. Having now recovered from the shock, I was taken up on to the platform and presented with a cheque and was assured that everyone in the place had contributed.

The microphone was placed in my hand and I proceeded to relate the fact that I had been promised a fantastic meal in a wonderful hotel, "but instead I have found myself here, with you lot and a plateful of sandwiches!" I'm happy to say everyone was amused. I thanked them profoundly, and all had a good time. One last surprise was yet to come; someone passed me a mobile phone, and I heard my son Teddy's voice all the way from Australia. It sounded like he was just around the corner, but I was very quickly assured that he was unable to be there. I knew he was with me in spirit, and one day I'm confident he will make his way home to us if only for a visit.

My story is coming to an end, but my life is not. I shall continue to write poetry and maybe I will write short stories. My love of life will ensure that I will reach out and embrace all that it has to offer me.

My family is my life's blood; I don't mother them, I just need to know they are there. I am content in the knowledge that I am truly loved and that I have earned their respect. I am indeed a very happy and contented woman, and my eye's are more open to what's around me than ever before in my life. Age is slowing me down, but it gives me more time to see things that I was always too busy to see when I was younger.

The world we live in, this wonderful planet, is a place so full of marvellous colour and energy – it is often a wild and uncontrolled force to have to deal with. The sheer wonder of the creation of life itself is beyond me. Sadly I believe the planet is being exploited, and if this doesn't stop, life itself at sometime in the future could perish.

We all should stop, and take the time to really see what we have all around us, and to realize how precious the gift of life is, and then contemplate the fact that stares us all in the face when we choose to see it: our time spent here comes only once, and death comes never late.

Christine

Me and Mary at my 70th birthday

TRANQUILLITY

I walk through the woods where the bluebells are growing,
There's a warm gentle breeze and my hearts overflowing,
Just wandering and thinking, so much on my mind,
No more peaceful way for relief will I find,
The Sun low in the sky as it slips towards night,
And the sunshine in shafts giving plenty of light,
Small creatures that scuttle and rustle through leaves,
The darting of bird and the humming of bees,
Many tall trees that offer me beauty and shade,
As I wound my way through this most beautiful glade,
As my mind wanders off and I savour this treat,
My heart settles down to a comfortable beat.

Rebecca Blakeley

Printed in the United Kingdom by
Lightning Source UK Ltd., Milton Keynes
140613UK00002BA/15/A